Walking With Chipeta

A 179 Year Journey through Chipeta's World to Mine

A Memoir by
Vickie Leigh Krudwig

Harmony House Art Studio
Westminster, Colorado
www.harmonyhousestudio.com

WALKING WITH CHIPETA
A 179 Year Journey through Chipeta's World to Mine

A memoir by Vickie Leigh Krudwig

Editors:

Susan Hill Newton
Faye Quam-Hemrl
Pat Hayward

Harmony House Art Studio
Westminster, CO
www.harmonyhousestudio.com

ISBN: 978-0-9700127-5-3

Library of
Congress Control
Number:
2022916567

Sometimes dreams are wiser than waking.

**Black Elk*

*Black Elk was an Oglala Sioux (ca. 1863-1950) Medicine Man and Spiritual Leader From the book, *Black Elk Speaks: The Life Story of a Holy Man of the Oglala Sioux*

Chapter One
The Dream

It was just before daybreak when I first heard her speak. "Come," she said, "follow me." I obeyed and effortlessly entered a misty world followed by an art gallery steeped in the scents of canvas, paint, and turpentine. The walls held paintings of haunting mountain landscapes with unfamiliar peaks and valleys. I turned from the paintings and looked with the eyes of a child through the gallery windows, where blue and lavender snow-capped peaks reached above a valley floor and into an azure sky. A brook undulated across a grassy meadow. An evocative flute melody floated toward me. A mountain breeze caressed my face while the earthy scent of damp moss and willows stirred a longing in me.

"Follow me," the woman whispered again. And she and I, unseen presence and sleeping dreamer, traveled as one through time and space into a weather-beaten, white clapboard house. The place was filled with foreboding. Even though dreaming, I told myself to memorize every detail. When I saw there were no signs of life, a chill took hold of every cell in my body. Over there was a window, its four panes rippled with age. Just below the window was a stack of food-encrusted plates which sat precariously on the edge of a counter. "Greed," I said to myself, eyeing the plates. "An unstoppable, gluttonous appetite." Beyond the window I saw nothingness, a bleak, bare, wintery nothingness that stretched to infinity. My heart lurched. "Watch," the woman said, her voice overriding my urge to turn away.

I do not know how long I watched before they appeared. Smokey forms emerged from the void; men, women, and children huddled under ragged shawls and blankets. Their hunched shoulders carried their broken spirits. More figures emerged. And then more. I closed my eyes. "Watch," the presence said firmly. I forced myself to keep looking. Beyond the people, I saw layers of blue and lavender mountains, the same colors as in the gallery, but not the same mountains I had seen earlier. I did not recognize them. I was drawn to them, and even felt homesick for them. *Who are these people?* I thought. *What do they want?* I did not know. *Where are they from?* Again, I did not know.

***The Dream.* Artwork by Vickie Leigh Krudwig. 2005.**

Suddenly, I understood: They were Indigenous people on a godforsaken reservation. The woman spoke firmly into my right ear. "Write my story," the presence said. And then … disappeared into the mist leading the others from my sleeping dream.

I jolted wide awake, my heart pounding. Then I lay in the darkness and trembled, the dream had upset me that much. As hard as I tried, I could not get back to sleep. I reached for my glasses and put them on. The clock on my husband's nightstand read 4:00 a.m. I lay my head back on the pillow, to try and regain my composure, but, like a slideshow, the images of my dream replayed themselves over and over. I needed to get up and write down this vision. Everything seemed important. I knew who the woman was. She was Chipeta. A member of the Tabeguache Ute Nation, born in 1843.

The house was still as I slipped into the kitchen. I put coffee on and while it brewed began to journal in haste. I wrote as fast as I could, trying to recall every detail of my dream. I filled page after page with words and rough sketches of what I had observed. Twelve pages later, I put my pen down and closed my journal. I stood up and stretched. I poured myself a hot cup of coffee and walked over to the patio door. I stared eastward, past rows of houses in our Denver neighborhood. Opening the door, I stepped out onto our deck and into the darkness. All was quiet and serene.

Shivering, I set my cup down on the railing and pulled my robe around me. The air was chilly and damp, and the morning stars still shone in the April sky. The dream hung heavily in my mind and heart. *Why me*? I wondered. *I am a white woman. I know little about Chipeta and her Ute tribe. Who am I to embark on such a project?* I was a children's author and illustrator, not a scholarly historian. All I knew about Chipeta, and the Ute, was what I had learned in childhood Colorado history lessons and the little I had written about her in my book, *Hiking through Colorado History*. In school, my history textbooks talked about the miners and pioneers coming to Colorado in the 1850s and how "The Ute were moved to make way for other things." This did not prepare me for what I was about to learn over the next few years. My childhood fantasy of a happy and peaceful Ute existence in Colorado would turn into an ugly reality.

I spent my childhood summers visiting places where the Ute had lived. I would watch in wonder as Ute drummers and dancers, dressed in their fine regalia, performed in the Garden of the Gods in Colorado Springs, Colorado. I also saw dancers and drummers in Manitou Springs, located alongside the old Ute Pass. Through my young eyes, they were magical and romantic. My father told my siblings and me about the Ute people. He said they once called Colorado home but had to leave the state to live on reservations. Where were the reservations? I did not know. I also had no understanding of what living on a reservation would have been like.

While arrowhead hunting with my siblings in the high mountain meadows near Buena Vista and Salida, Colorado, our father, through his storytelling, would paint vivid images of teepees set up along the nearby creek. Though invisible to me, I used to feel as though the Ute people were still there, watching me play in the long grasses, amongst the aspen trees. Standing on my deck now, I smiled at the memory.

Sounds of a stirring household pulled me from the past and into the present. I stepped back into the house. It was time to get kids ready for school and complete household tasks plus work on my writing and illustrating projects. They were fiction based and less fearsome than my dream, which would have to wait. Truth be told, I was not sure I wanted to know more about the people in the dream. I was afraid of what I might learn.

Chapter Two
I'm Not Angry

It had been three weeks since I had first dreamed about Chipeta, a Ute woman born more than a century earlier, who had unexpectedly come to me one morning just before dawn. I had promised Chipeta and her Ute Ancestors that I would write her story; it was time I committed to it. I would head down to the History Colorado Center in Denver, Colorado to begin my research. My heart and intuition had made the decision for me. I know I had to leave the comfort of my world and learn about hers. I committed to praying and meditating in the early mornings and often in the evenings. I kept my journal next to the bed, so I could capture the messages in my dreams by recording them exactly as they came to me.

These journal entries created comfort and often conflict within me. I was being asked to examine the inside *and* outside of my own life. This forced me to dig below the rock-hard surface of my soul and confront my past and the experiences that had made me fearful and full of grief. I started to remember the "good, the bad, and the ugly," and began accepting that the effects of them were part of my life's journey.

My journals were filled with entries about wonderful events, dreams for my future, lamentations of lost opportunities, loss of identity and self, about fear of the future, fear of the past, and even fear of my present life. My twin, Veronica, said I acted angry when I talked about my past. I would smile and say, "I am not angry," but my journal pages told the truth: I was *filled* with rage.

Hurtful and life-changing experiences often revealed themselves through my journaling. As a child I experienced sexual abuse by family friends. Then there was physical and emotional abuse from those I loved and revered. In my early adulthood, I watched in horror as my former brother-in-law tried to beat my sister to death on a cold, gray November afternoon. I also remembered the deep, deep agony I experienced losing two babies early in my pregnancies. I never spoke of this heartache I felt. It was my fault for being a failure as a woman. No one in my family talked of such things.

The memories came in a torrent. Like a flash flood, there was no stopping them, though I tried at times. I stayed busy helping everyone else, volunteering for all kinds of activities and committees at school and church. As my children grew older, I started my own businesses. I spent money at thrift shops, searched for "beautiful things" to make our home or myself more presentable. I would still feel empty. My husband and I argued over the finances, making me want to run away and leave my life behind. When my kids became more independent and started to leave home, the hole in my heart became a crater. I needed to go to counseling.

I'd been in counseling before, after my brother, George, and his wife, Cheryl, lost their twin daughters late in Cheryl's pregnancy. At the twins' funeral, thinking about losing my own babies overwhelmed me, and I wept: for the twins, for my brother and his wife, and for my unborn babies. Afterward my brother and his wife sent me a check and suggested I use it for counseling. It was one of the greatest gifts I've ever received.

Chapter Three
Into the Unknown

White-knuckled, I gripped the steering wheel with both hands and inched my way up the steep and icy road, US Highway 40, to Berthoud Pass. I was driving home to Denver after giving a Colorado history presentation at a school in Granby, Colorado. Another spring storm had brought light snows, which covered the roadway in a blanket of white, making me struggle to maintain my composure as I crept forward. I also had something other than the weather on my mind. I kept asking myself how I could confess to my mom, who was with me, that my life was out of control.

I scolded myself for announcing to the children and teachers at that Grandby school that I was going to write about Chipeta and the Ute. I did not know how it happened. I hadn't *planned* to say it. It just came out of my mouth. Teachers were thrilled, saying they needed more Colorado history books for children. It had been less than a month since I had the dream about Chipeta. In front of more than 400 people I had gone and committed myself to doing this. I hated letting anyone down, so I could not back out of it. I knew I would have to research Chipeta's life and times and write about them. It was the least I could do.

It had taken me seven years and hundreds of submissions to publishers to achieve my dream of becoming a children's author and illustrator, but in 1996 through 1999, two publishers in Colorado bought my books. In addition, I had published short stories in *Highlights for*

Children and *Wild Outdoor World Magazine*. My first picture book, *Cucumber Soup*, was nominated for a Benjamin Franklin Book Award and was a finalist for the Florida Children's Book Award. *Hiking through Colorado History*, a brief history of Colorado and its People, was also successful. I was traveling all over Colorado, giving paid presentations about my books, and making a good income. All of this was thrilling.

I was a successful published author, so why was I beginning to feel as though I were someone else? I was no longer the Vickie I knew. I was identifying with being an author and illustrator, which made me feel important and that I had accomplished something that I hoped would please my husband, my children, my parents, and my in-laws. My name appearing in newspaper articles, my receiving awards, and attending book signings made me feel even more important. But the truth was, I was afraid I was a fraud. I did not have a formal degree, so I worried all the time about the critics and what they would say. More importantly what would my family think of my success? When I called my parents to tell them I had sold my first two books to publishers, my dad's response was, "You really know how to BS your way into things." While he might have been trying to be funny, his comment set a precedence for how I would feel throughout my career as a writer.

In the past I had started businesses all on my own, with limited financial support. There just was not any extra money once my husband and I had taken care of household expenses. I made strides, but I also failed miserably. I had no business experience, so I would find business partners who promised me large incomes generated by my ideas and products, but these partners would prove unethical and greedy. They would leave me with little income while they lined their own pockets. I loved getting their approval for my creativity, so I often took them at their flattering word. I hoped I would fill my bank account with the thousands they had promised. Then I could show everyone that I was worthy and smart. They would see I was not a complete and utter failure.

Mark, my husband, warned me about these too-good-to-be-true ventures. I did not want to hear his input. I took his concerns and suggestions as criticisms and ignored them. Still, he would try, as much as he was able, to support my risky endeavors. This made me feel guilty that he had to work so hard to earn a steady income for our family of five.

The more I tried and failed with businesses and projects, the more despair I felt. Debts piled up, and creditors would call asking for their money. Out of shame and fear, I hid my business debts from my husband. I was afraid he would grow too frustrated with my failures and leave me. He never did. When my secrets about my business became too much and I felt remorse, I would confess to my debts, cry, and ask him for financial help. It was a pattern I would often repeat throughout the years.

I believe my anxiety and fear started when I was a young child of seven or eight. As an adult I would remember my mom's fear and her anger at my dad when finances were tight. I was aware at that tender age that we could lose our home because of a missed mortgage payment. By the time I was 10, I had jobs and would often help my parents out if they needed a little money. Sometimes I bought my own clothes. It was clear then that having lots of money meant safety, enough food and clothing, and making people happy. I left home at eighteen, to make my own way in the world. I was proud I was financially stable and independent. Now, as an adult, it would have been selfish for me to save the money I had earned while others went without food or a roof over their head. I sometimes downplayed the amount of money I gave away.

After Mark and I faced two long-lasting layoffs, our money situation became entangled with my self-worth—

Mark's self-worth, too, I am sure. He hated being unable to provide for our family. While we took three years to climb out of what seemed like a bottomless pit of debts, I would constantly look for ways to help pay the bills. I was like my dad. He had lots of creative ideas for products and companies but never enough capital or business acumen to keep them alive. He would struggle and fail and eventually sell his companies, just to make ends meet for his family of seven.

My conscience was conflicted over my need for parental approval and my immediate family's financial needs. This contributed to my anxiety. I felt like I was "damned" if I gave away my earnings and "damned" if I did not. I know now that my Catholic upbringing also played a part in this. I learned "it is better to give than to receive," especially if I wanted to get to heaven. I felt guilty for being successful and having money. How could I keep this money for myself when my parents and siblings were struggling?

I began having full-blown anxiety attacks and insomnia. One relentlessly fed the other. When these attacks became too prominent in my life, my doctor prescribed medication to help me sleep at night. Without it, I would lay trembling in bed under the cover of darkness, afraid to close my eyes. I had become obsessed with dying. (I was already dying … inside.) No one could save me from myself, and my ensuing panic attacks. Mark would try to reassure me that I was okay, but I'd insist we go to the emergency room, anyway, because I had chest pains and shortness of breath. He grew frustrated when we would go, and the doctors would check and recheck me and find nothing wrong with me. These trips to the emergency room were costly, too. These attacks affected my relationship with Mark and with my children.

Despite my shaky mental health, my writing continued, and my books sold well. I booked programs for several schools a month, and they always went well. I illustrated and helped design books for other authors who were independently publishing their own books. This meant I had a steady stream of income coming in. I looked like I had it all, and I did, plus an anxiety disorder. I would arrive at a school or an event, looking confident and full of energy, when just an hour earlier I would have been fighting the urge to cancel the program and stay home. I felt safer there. If I traveled out of town for a school presentation, I would always bring my mom or my children with me. I was afraid to go anywhere alone. I needed them in case something happened to me.

On top of my anxiety disorder, my dream of Chipeta and her request that I write her story were ever-present. I really did want to write her story but thinking about doing it justice terrified me. I had never written a scholarly biography. I was not sure I could. There were already books about the Ute people on the market. I was afraid mine would not stand up to them. Why did I tell the students in Grandby that I was going to write Chipeta's story?

I reached the summit of Berthoud Pass (11,307 ft.), where the snow continued to fall. It was time to drive down the other side of the mountain. Though it was cold outside, beads of perspiration formed on my forehead. As I slowly made my way down the pass, I watched in horror as cars in front of me slipped sideways on the snow and ice. The sides of the mountains were steep and frightening. I kept my eyes on the road and my hands tightly wrapped around the wheel. I had no idea what waited beyond the next curve. Likewise, I had no idea what waited around the next curve on the highway of my life. I had no concept of what that first dream meant and what I was supposed to do with it, or me with my own life, for that matter. I was traveling unknown territory. I knew I needed to find out who I was as a person. My life depended on it.

I survived this treacherous drive over Berthoud Pass and was glad to get back to my routines at home. However, three weeks later, I decided it would not hurt to visit the History Colorado Center and check out their materials on Chipeta and the Ute tribe. I arrived with a tablet and pencils in hand and made my request. A staff member gave me a pair of white cotton gloves and led me to a table in the library. An attendant brought me boxes, manilla envelopes, and folders to go through.

I carefully picked up a manilla envelope containing photographs, opened it, pulled out a photo, and stiffened. The woman in the photo was the woman I had dreamed about, Chipeta. The black and white image from 1909 showed her in her later years, standing alongside baskets, her faced etched with lines formed over her long life. I could not help wondering what she'd been thinking the moment the photographer took this picture. Her dark eyes gazed into mine and a shiver ran through me.

One of the first photos I saw in the archive folders. Chipeta's eyes seemed to stare into mine. Chipeta in 1909. **Photographer: by Thomas J. McKee. Denver Public Library, Western History Collection. (Z1457).**

There were other photos of Chipeta and her husband, Ouray, during the Brunot Treaty talks with the United States government in 1873. In those photos she was quite young. I learned it was unusual for women to participate in council meetings. These and other images represented specific times in Chipeta's life. Looking at them, I felt an inexplicable, immediate connection to and admiration for Chipeta.

Next, I opened Works Progress Administration (WPA) files, which held typed interviews of people who'd known

Chipeta. During his presidency, Franklin D. Roosevelt created the WPA to help Americans get back to work and on their feet following the Great Depression. WPA projects included infrastructure, building schools and hospitals, upgrading highways and byways, building trails and visitor centers in national parks, and other beneficial programs. One project was recording American history through interviews and art, which employed writers and fine artists.

The WPA files had numerous interviews and stories about Chipeta and Ute people. The writing on the now yellowed onionskin paper held me spellbound. I read accounts of Chipeta's generosity and compassion for others, about the ways she'd helped settlers in need, shared food with the hungry, and taken care of children in her tribes. One WPA account said she played guitar for her guests. Another mentioned she once had a pet mountain lion that, undoubtably, startled her visitors. One of my favorite accounts concerned Chipeta gathering children around her, patting her lap, and saying, "Come, children, let me tell you a story." I loved that she was a storyteller and so kind and giving to others.

The more I read, the more I wanted to write Chipeta's story. I ordered copies of photos and historical documents and took them home. When I re-read each document, I felt a pull that was stronger than my fear or anxiety, so I decided right then and there that I would at least take the first step and gather more details about Chipeta, and I would map a preliminary plan for her book. This meant I would have to take my search for her beyond the comfort of the History Colorado Center, the Western History Collection at the Denver Public Library, and my home.

Chapter Four
Waiting for Affirmation

Women played a crucial role in the well-being of Chipeta's tribe. They made clothing and tools for everyday use, found plants for food and medicine, set up camps, and cared for the children and elders. At around eight years of age, Chipeta's mother would have given her a digging stick used to uproot and harvest a variety of plants. Her mother, grandmother, and aunts would have taught Chipeta to identify important plants, their purpose, when to pick them, and how to store them. When I was young, my father taught me about growing plants. In the spring we would sow green beans, carrots, tomatoes, and corn. Later in the summer, he would celebrate the harvest with our family and friends.

By playing with toys representing tools the women used, Chipeta may have learned how to dress hides, sew clothes, and take care of children. I smiled when I read this in my research, because as a child I loved taking care of my dolls. My mom showed me how to diaper them and how to feed and burp them. She had even put powdered milk in a doll bottle for me. I played with a toy iron, with little pots and pans and dishes, and with a tiny broom. Like Chipeta, I learned to sew. My mom and older sister, Valorie, taught me how to sew simple things like bean bags and tiny drawstring purses.

By the time I was twelve, they had taught me how to cook full meals, and when my dad praised my "delicious" fried chicken, I would beam with pride. These were life skills I passed along to my children. It was crucial for

Chipeta and the tribe's children to learn these life skills too. It was a matter of survival should they ever be separated from the tribe.

My collection of documents and photos grew. I pored through files at the Western History Collection at the Denver Public Library and at the archives from the History Colorado Center.

Unfortunately, the more I read, the more disquieted I became. Pastoral photos of the Ute sitting in front of teepees, gathered with family or community, gave way to images of brutal reservation life. Eerily, some images looked like the view from the window in my first dream about Chipeta.

Except for the few I had passed through while on family vacations, reservations were unfamiliar to me. I did not understand what it meant to live on them and that government treaties forced millions of men, women, and children to leave their homelands and live on reservations. The government repeated this process from coast to coast. It was disgraceful. I witnessed this through the black and white, and sometimes sepia, prints in the folders. The images did not lie.

Life on the reservation was harsh. I vacillated between writing Chipeta's book and turning my attention elsewhere, because I did not know how to deal with this information. It overwhelmed me and filled me with grief for Chipeta, the Ute, and for the other Indigenous tribes across the country. *How can I use words to accurately portray this kind of suffering and injustice?*

I saw that racial bias fueled the push to assimilate Indigenous people across our country and around the world into a non-Indigenous culture. This assimilation was supposed to "save" the Indigenous men, women, and their children.

Where were the stories and histories written by the Ute? Their histories, I would later learn, were from the oral tradition of storytelling. This was how the tribes kept their history alive. It seemed to me, many of the writers in the 1800s and early 1900s were non-Indigenous historians who did not fully grasp the lives and cultures of Indigenous nations. Sometimes the men who, as military leaders, forced Indigenous people off their homelands and onto reservations, were the ones who wrote books about the Ute and other Indigenous cultures. Publishers often thought Indian Agency employees (government employees who managed the reservations) were experts on the Indigenous way of life.

I could not count on these books presenting Indigenous people in a positive light. History books written from the late 1800s through the early 1900s frequently used disparaging words to describe them, words such "heathens" and "noble savages." In the mid-1800s, these descriptions flooded newspaper articles and not only indoctrinated readers into a romanticized Wild West version of western expansion but also encouraged hatred for the tribes still living in their traditional homelands, lands coveted by the settlers and the United States government.

As I perused these files, I was aware that authors rarely wrote about Indigenous women. There were first-hand accounts about them in the WPA files, but most scholars chose to ignore them. If they did write about women, they wrote exaggerated tales from a non-Indigenous perspective. Newspaper man and poet, Eugene Field, penned a romantic and racially biased poem entitled "Chipeta," following the Meeker Incident in 1879. "She is the bravest and best of a cursed race," begins the poem. "She rode where old Ouray dare not ride…." This inaccurately tells readers that Ouray was not brave enough to ride through the wilderness to help rescue the Meeker women. The truth was, Ouray was quite ill with Bright's Disease, known today as kidney nephritis. He did not just passively step aside. He helped with negotiations and sent tribesmen to help release the women. And once the women were free, Chipeta and Ouray welcomed them into their home, took care of them, and listened while the women recounted what happened during their captivity. Witnesses said Chipeta wept bitterly for them.

Eugene Field and other newspaper men began to call Chipeta "Queen of the Utes," which like most kids growing up in Colorado, was all I had ever remembered about her. No one ever told me what all these events were about. Worse, they never told us about the forced removal of the Ute and other tribes from their traditional homelands.

The dreams of Chipeta persisted for over a year. She seemed determined that I write on her behalf. But like in the movies, I wanted a clear and tangible sign, that I had permission to write her biography. I wanted an *undeniable* sign, so I could move forward. We humans seem to need proof. We do not trust the visions, even when our hearts already know what they are telling us to do. We want concrete proof we're going to do the right thing.

I always believed that I was a spiritual person because of my childhood teachings from the Catholic and Methodist churches. This awareness had reached a higher level. These new Indigenous spiritual experiences made me feel calm and centered. I felt protected and certain about my journey. Was the energy I now felt Chipeta's spirit, or that of her Ancestors? I did not know for sure. I only knew that when they were present, the hair on my head and arms stood up, and shivers ran throughout my entire body.

In mid-summer I took a break from my research to clear my head. My kids and I visited my parents who lived in a small, refurbished bunkhouse, twenty miles south of Colorado Springs. As I stood outside their home, I studied the red rock formations and groves of juniper spread across the land.

I looked skyward and silently asked Chipeta for a sign that I was on the right road. It might have seemed a bit dramatic. I had to justify my obsession with her. I already knew I could not depend on information from the early history books written by non-Indigenous authors long ago. While I appreciated the efforts of twentieth century writers who'd authored books about the Ute and other tribes, I knew I needed a tribal—direct—perspective on Chipeta's life and times. I would have to travel and come face-to-face with her descendants, her history, and, in the process, come face-to-face with my own fears. I was afraid I would dig up more mournful history than I could handle. I must admit, I was also worried about being a non-Indigenous person. How would her descendants receive me?

I inhaled and offered a brief prayer to Chipeta or whoever else might be listening. Asking for signs came from my years growing up Catholic. God gave saints amazing signs to acknowledge their definite role in a situation. I scanned the skies, waited. The air was still. The only sounds were the grating of cicadas and clicking of grasshoppers. "Please, Grandmother," I whispered. "I want to write your story, but I'm afraid." My pulse raced, and tears filled my eyes. I searched the horizon and the red rocks for a sign. I had no idea what it would be. I just wanted proof that I was on the right path.

Later that day, my kids and I, along with my six-year-old niece and eight-year-old nephew, my dad, mom, and siblings took a hike to explore the area behind my parents' home. My siblings and I had learned early to watch for stone artifacts that could have been from Ute, Cheyenne, Arapaho, or other Indigenous tribes who once traveled throughout the Rocky Mountain region. As young as three years old, we learned to find and identify flint chips, small bird points, and scrapers as we made our way over the rocky terrain near our cabin in Nathrop, Colorado.

I lagged on the hike, as I loved the solitude of walking alone. Truthfully, I was waiting for my sign. I walked past a grove of piñon trees, which I imagined Chipeta and other women and children spreading blankets under. They would gently shake the boughs of the trees, to release the nutrient rich nuts to fall into the folds of their blankets. They were careful to leave plenty of piñon nuts for the birds and other animals dependent upon them for food. Chipeta's past felt palpable in this landscape.

"Here, Aunt Vickie, this is for you," my niece said, interrupting my thoughts and running straight for me. She was clasping something in her hand. I thought she held the usual child's gift: a rock, a pinecone, or a flint chip. I smiled and opened my right hand to receive it. She placed in my palm something resembling a bird bone, five inches long and pointed at one end. It was old and worn, stained red from the earth. I turned it over and gasped. It was a woman's bone awl, a tool used by Indigenous people to punch holes into leather when making clothes or other useful items such as leather bags and parfleches. I had seen similar tools in books during my research.

"Where did you find this?" I asked.

My niece pointed to a spot on the ground ten feet away. I wondered how it got there. The area was well known for flash flooding during heavy rainstorms, for water sweeping down the rocky slopes, through the trees, and down the creek bed. Perhaps it had been swept down by a the rain. "You are supposed to have it," she insisted.

"Are you sure you do not want to keep it?"

"No. It is yours," she said matter-of-factly before trotting off to join the other hikers.

I pressed the awl to my chest. "I will tell your story," I whispered to Chipeta.

Chapter Five

Making the Connection-Ute Indian Museum

When I returned to Denver, I began my work in earnest. I organized three-ring binders, made timelines, and put my materials in order. I laid the bone awl, which I would later learn was hundreds of years old, in a place of honor on my desk, along with other objects meant to inspire me. My preparations complete, it was time to contact the Ute Indian Museum in Montrose, Colorado. It sits on land the United States government had allotted to Ouray and Chipeta. It was where the couple had built their adobe home near the Uncompahgre River. They raised crops and tended sheep, as suggested by the United States government, and strove to fit into the community, sometimes by entertaining white settlers in their home. They wanted peace with them, but, sadly, newcomers were jealous of their success. So, they complained to United States government officials that the Ute were stealing food out of the mouths of white people. Eventually, and after Ouray died, the United States government auctioned off Chipeta and Ouray's home and land and gave it to someone else.

I found the museum's phone number. Apprehensive and excited, I called. "Good morning. Ute Indian Museum," a woman said. "This is CJ speaking."

I had visited the Ute Indian Museum only one time, in 1982, while on vacation with my husband and our six-month-old daughter, and I had not given it another thought. I had always liked history, and this had been another interesting stop on our trip, nothing more. And now it was February 2002.

I liked the curator, CJ Brafford, the moment I heard her singsong voice over the phone. I could hear her smile. Using my most professional voice, I explained that the purpose of my call was to learn more about Chipeta and her people. I did not tell CJ about my dream, of course. What would she have thought of me?

CJ listened carefully and then recommended that I visit the museum. My stomach lurched. Travel. I would have to drive to Montrose. "There are files full of documents that may help you with your research," she said. We talked more, and then she recommended that I call Chipeta's great, great grandson, O. Roland McCook, Sr. He lived in Fort Duchesne, Utah, near the Uintah-Ouray Reservation. "He might be willing to help you," she said.

My mind reeled. I had thought I would just use research to write a quick book, travel to promote it, and then be done with it. But then I felt Chipeta's call to go to Montrose. It felt like a longing to "come home." I had not expected this strong of a connection to Chipeta. I had not anticipated that I would meet her descendant. I also had not expected that I would soon travel in Utah, New Mexico, and other places in Colorado, pursuing her history.

I dutifully wrote down Roland's number on the tablet in front of me and thanked CJ for her time. I set the receiver down and stared into space. Things were already getting complicated. I did not want to wait to call Roland, as I was afraid if I did, I would lose my courage. With a twinge of nervousness, I picked up the phone, dialed. He answered immediately. "This is Roland."

I quickly introduced myself to Chipeta's *great, great grandson.* I explained that I was interested in writing a biography about Chipeta.

"Well, everyone wants to write about her," he said curtly. "We will see. I need to think about it." He hung up. *Okay. What will I do if he says no? I need to write this book.* I had promised Chipeta I would.

Over the next few days, I busied myself with projects and household tasks. Then came the voice in my head, another gentle nudge from Chipeta. Her thoughts had permeated mine. *Tell Roland about the dream,* she said. The message was clear and concise. I groaned inwardly, yet I knew that I had to do as she requested. I decided to wait a day before I talked to Roland again, because I was afraid of how he might react. I'd call CJ first and tell her about my dream.

"This may sound strange," I said. "I did not tell you everything when I called you three days ago. You see, I had this dream..."

CJ listened patiently as I described the dream and its myriad details. She surprised me by saying, "That does not sound strange at all. Seven years ago, I felt the call to come to the museum." She said I should call Roland immediately and tell him about the dream.

I hung up. I closed my eyes. I took a deep breath. Shaking, I picked up the phone and dialed Roland's number. The phone rang three times and then the answering machine picked up. I was both disappointed and relieved. "Roland, this is Vickie Leigh Krudwig, again. I'm sorry to bother you, but..." I babbled at length about my dream. Then I left my telephone number and hung up.

What will this man think? He's a Tribal Chairman of the Northern Ute, for heaven's sake! I paced in my office. I imagined the police or FBI coming to my house and arresting me for stalking. "I watch too many movies," I said to myself.

Then anxiety took over. *What the hell do you think you are doing?* my inner critic raged. *You cannot do this.* And then… the phone rang. I froze. I knew who it was. I

If the Walls Could Talk. Artwork by Vickie Leigh Krudwig, 2006.

slowly picked up the receiver. "Hello?" I said, my voice was trembling.

"This is Roland McCook. I am supposed to help you."

Weak kneed, I plopped into a chair. *Oh my God* I thought, *this cannot be happening*. Roland explained that my dream contained things that few people knew about. I'd mentioned the dishes inside the whitewashed building, the people huddled outside, and an old stone pipe. Funny thing is, I don't remember how I knew about the pipe.

"I will do everything I can to help you," Roland said, his voice softer and kinder than it was during our first call. I could hardly grasp this. In an instant, the world I had known had radically shifted. I would not turn my back on Chipeta now, which meant I would have to push aside my feelings of inadequacy and shove my inner critic out of my head. I would trust the process and trust in myself and my abilities as a writer.

I told Roland about my plans to travel to Montrose to visit the Ute Indian Museum in late April. Unfortunately, his schedule was full, so he would not be able to meet me there. He said he would ask CJ to help me with research materials. Even though I was disappointed I could not meet him, I was still grateful he was willing to provide support during the project.

In mid-March, I contacted Fulcrum Publishing in Golden, Colorado, and arranged a meeting. Fulcrum had published my picture book, *Cucumber Soup*, in 1998. I presented my proposal for Chipeta's biography to the editor and the marketing department, and they accepted the proposal, no questions asked. I needed Roland McCook's formal blessing before I could start writing, so I told them this. I hoped they would be willing to wait. Thankfully, they were.

Thinking about my conversation with Roland later, it struck me that he never once asked who I was or what I did for a living. Was he aware I was a white woman? If he was, he did not say. (He would later call me *Americat Mamutch,* American Woman.) He simply acknowledged my dream and the journey I was about to undertake.

Chapter Six

A New Car and a Celestial Meeting

I continued to assemble my collection of historical items about Chipeta. The more I learned the more intrigued I grew. Her life began in a Tabeguache village in the vicinity of Conejos, Colorado, in June of 1843. There are some historians who tell a different story.

They say that as a child Chipeta was the sole survivor of a raid in a Kiowa and Apache camp. She was born at a time when trappers and traders had been steadily making their way into the Rocky Mountains to exploit natural resources vital to Indigenous people living in the region. Fur traders, greedy for beaver and buffalo pelts, trapped or outright slaughtered animals to near extinction. Ouray, Chipeta's future husband, was born in November 1833, during the Leonid meteor showers seen by the tribe as a good sign for leadership. Both he and Chipeta would go on to play pivotal leadership roles in the Ute tribe.

Although this was only a portion of what I would learn about Chipeta, it got so I thought about her and the Ute people day and night. Never had one of my projects consumed me so totally. I crammed my journals full of words I hoped would capture the feelings she evoked in me. I wrote poetry and drew sketches to express the intensity of my emotions. Sometimes vivid dreams jolted me out of bed and onto the couch in our family room.

In these dreams ancient voices whispered urgent messages meant to instruct me and move me forward. It was supernatural. I kept these dreams to myself, as I was afraid my family, friends, and fellow church members would criticize me.

When I did tell people, they acted a bit concerned and sympathetic. One person suggested I was in the middle of a nervous breakdown. A church friend warned me that Indigenous spirituality was a dangerous cult. What this person did not know was, even before the first dream, I had already been connected to the spiritual world of Indigenous cultures and had always felt a deep longing when I read about Indigenous people or watched television programs about them.

My in-laws were uneasy with my connection to the spiritual realm of the Indigenous cultures. My own mother and father simply listened and then changed the subject. They were concerned about the changes in my spirituality. Longtime members of the A.A. and Al-Anon twelve-step programs, my parents recommended that I needed a spiritual program such as the twelve-step program or church. Mark was skeptical about my beliefs. He was a scientist and a logical thinker who did not believe in the supernatural. Mystical happenings like mine made him roll his eyes or simply sigh. He was clearly uncomfortable with my revelations about my dreams and visions. It made me feel ambivalent toward Mark, as I couldn't share the real me with him.

And yet… my twin sister, Veronica, and my older sister, Valorie, listened with fascination. *They* believed me. My oldest daughter, Jessica, and my youngest child, Benjamin, also believed me and in my connection with Chipeta. I sensed they that they, too, had mystical connections with the world around them. My middle daughter, Rebecca, analytical like Mark, was hesitantly supportive.

Because Colorado's high mountain passes can be unpredictable and unforgiving during the winter, I made the commitment to drive over to Montrose in late April. Spring blizzards were less likely then. The very thought of travel scared and thrilled me at the same time. To make this journey, though, I needed reliable transportation, a new car. I could rent one, but then I would have to rent again, and again. It did not make sense.

In the months before this trip came up, I had mentioned more than once to Mark that we needed to purchase a second car. Our kids were now nineteen, fifteen, and twelve, and I was getting tired of driving them around all the time. Plus, I did not want to be stuck at home if Mark or one of the kids needed our only car. But Mark would always say it was not a good time to spend the money, so I would drop it. We had just celebrated our twenty-fifth wedding anniversary, and things were going well in our relationship. I would tell myself I was happy. But I was not. I could not let it go, and it saddened me. I would vent my frustration in my journals.

The more I thought about needing a car, the more angst I felt. Mark and I had always made big purchases together, but now I was contemplating buying one by myself. *Why couldn't I make a purchase like this by myself? Didn't Mark trust me to do it?* I became depressed, and a male doctor wanted to prescribe medicine that would make me numb but happier. I listened to my inner voice and wanted to refuse. I didn't. I filled the prescription.

Then panic replaced my disappointment about the car. I was afraid I would completely fall back on old patterns and become anxious about everything and anything again or worry that I would die in my sleep. The patterns and habits were already creeping back, as I could see I was trying to suit the needs and expectations of the people around me but not trying to suit my own needs and expectations. Part of me knew I surely would die if I returned to my former way of life.

I called Valorie and visited with her for a long while. I had a successful greeting card line at the time, Naughty Pine Greetings. I had designed great cards and was selling them in the largest national parks across the country. I told her I was struggling and had once again trusted a man to make decisions for me. The owner of the wholesale company I worked with to sell my cards had promised me thousands of dollars in sales if I would give him exclusive rights to use my artwork and product line. He also asked me to copy other artists' concepts so he could have similar product lines. I refused. Then this unscrupulous businessman had an artist copy *my* art instead.

I felt furious and sad about this but took no action. I did not like conflict, and I was fearful of backlash. Once again, I would let it drop. "This is still another failure," I told my sister. "I am done trusting people and hoping they will do the right thing. And..., I took a deep breath, "After all the work I have put in, I deserve a new car!"

Valorie reminded me that I was not a failure and that I did not need to prove myself to anybody.

March 15, 2002

I am a courageous and victorious person and will sell my company. I will get my car! I have no doubt about it. I am going to quit worrying about what others think I should be doing or not doing. I am fully qualified to make my own decisions! I can make a living with my talents and abilities. I am a strong person, an experienced soul who knows things intuitively, yet keeps seeking answers from people who are closed minded. I must follow my heart. I must listen to the wisdom of my soul. I must do what I need to do to heal my heart and soul. God, I am so grateful for this insight. I struggle to live up to the "right" way of religion, yet I know your grace is upon me and goes beyond comprehension. We humans cannot fathom the depth of this world and the way in which we can experience it. God, I love you, and I accept complete healing from you. I am ready to live, love, and laugh. I am ready to take my life into my own hands and live according to my own spiritual needs. I offer myself, using my talents and abilities to tell the stories that can change a life. I give you my writing and illustrations and lift them up so they may be used for a higher purpose and soothe the souls of others. Thank you for the insights and wisdom, and for the pain that pushed me forward. I love you and I am so grateful.

Oh, kind daughter, the darkness of the world is a manmade thing. Ego, greed, prejudice, and fear all keep humans from reaching their fullest potential and their own divine purpose. The very things you experienced this week are the things you need, to understand your true nature. You look to men and women who are limited in their knowledge, yet do not trust the wisdom of your own soul. It isn't necessary to prove your worth, for it goes against the grain to fight for position.

***Sacred Moment*. Artwork by Vickie Leigh Krudwig, 2021.**

Simply live each day with purpose, love, compassion, and passion. Use your gifts to tell the story of love—to encourage others, and to simply let your soul celebrate its very existence on this Earth. That is celebration enough! Trust the universe, trust in Me in all matters. The world is about to unfold like a rosebud as it blooms. Rejoice and open to your own natural beauty—inside and out! You are talented and creative, and you will use them (talents and abilities) to inspire and to live a life of authenticity. Do not be afraid. Enjoy.

Two days before my trip, I decided to move forward on a car. I approached Mark about purchasing a car on my own, and he quickly brought up my less than stellar credit score. "You are not likely to get a loan," he said. His comment made me even more determined, so I covertly applied for a car loan and, despite my credit score, got approved, which amazed and thrilled me. Suddenly I was feeling in control of my life. While Mark was at work, I secretly visited car dealerships, where I made it clear to the salespeople that I did not want them hounding me while I looked. I alone would decide on the right vehicle for me and my budget. I had succinctly communicated my expectations without feeling nervous or guilty. It may sound silly, but this was a major milestone for me.

I was going to purchase my first car, a beautiful dark blue Dodge Neon. I left our old car at the dealership while I drove my new one home for a test drive. Later that day, I walked to the bus stop to meet Mark. I wanted to prepare him for what he was about to see: a new car, my car, sitting in the driveway.

Other than, "I am not happy about this," Mark said little when I told him. I knew he was disappointed in me and angry I hadn't included him in such a big decision. I had ignored his reasoning. He grudgingly rode in the Neon to the dealership to pick up our car. When we arrived, he got out and stood next to our car and asked in a clipped voice, "Are you coming?" Of course, his question really was, would I be a good wife and partner and come home with him, without a new car?

It was now our never. "No," I replied, after which I felt like I would drop to the asphalt. I looked right at him as I said, "I have to do the paperwork for my new car." Mark said nothing else. He got in our car and drove away.

My heart pounded so hard I thought it would explode when the salesman handed me my car keys. I drove into the night toward home. As I pulled into the driveway, I knew I had reached the point of no return. I suddenly felt both bold and shocked. I could hardly believe I had done this. I had purchased my ride to a new kind of independence. Did this scare Mark as much as it did me? Was he fearful I would leave and not come back? I did not know.

Now I had no more excuses for staying safe and comfortable at home. I could leave home and travel across the Rockies in pursuit of Chipeta. Better yet, I would not have to feel guilty for leaving Mark and the kids stranded because I had taken our only car for a trip. I would not have to worry about getting a rental car back to the rental lot on time.

My children were thrilled we would have another car in our household. They supported this part of my journey and encouraged me forward—something I had always tried to do for them. They were old enough to take care of themselves while I was away, so I did not have to fuss about leaving them. My in-laws had already expressed disapproval when I had traveled and left my husband and children behind. I guessed that when they and my parents learned about my purchase, they would all think I had mentally crossed the line. Was I being selfish, to make such a bold decision by myself? I did not think about Mark's needs. But I had to have my reliable and safe car for the trips I would take to uncover Chipeta's past. *I'm selfish. No, I'm not.*

It's done. I'd secured credit and signed the documents. I had become a renegade woman! I was thrilled, and it scared the hell out of me.

Mark said little to me when I climbed into bed that night. Exhausted and anxious, I popped a tranquilizer into my mouth. (I could not sleep without the tiny white pills I had become dependent on.) My body shuddered in the darkness, so I pulled the covers tightly around myself and waited for the pill's mind-numbing effect. *What is wrong with me*? *Why is this project so important?* I asked myself. I stared at the ceiling. *Am I crazy*? Who knew what was going to happen with all of this? In the morning I would put my suitcases in my new car and drive south to Colorado Springs to pick up my mother, who would accompany me on this trip. Valorie would drive up from Draper, Utah, and meet us in Montrose. Plans reviewed, I rolled over and whispered the urgent plea, "Please protect me," and then I fell into a deep sleep.

***Open Channels.* Artwork by Vickie Leigh Krudwig, 2022.**

Around 4:00 a.m., almost a year since the first dream of Chipeta, I woke with a start and saw a short of stature man and woman standing only inches from my bed. They were unearthly and bathed in a blue-white light. Hoping they were just part of another crazy dream, or an effect from taking the tranquilizer, I yanked the covers over my head, counted to three and then pulled the covers down. They were still there.

Amused by my childish reaction, the couple silently leaned forward and studied me. Then they looked at one another, nodded, and smiled. I closed my eyes for a second, and when I opened them again, they had vanished. I lay there and had the preposterous thought that they were Chipeta and Ouray. *They came to meet me before I drive to Montrose.* Oddly, I found great comfort in this thought. I felt they would protect me on my trip. After this, I was certain this book project was not going to be ordinary, it was going to be a life-changing affair. I smiled and fell into a peaceful sleep.

In the morning Mark helped me carry my luggage out to the car. Feeling horrendously guilty, I tried to keep things cheerful. I wanted to appear confident about my decision, even though I desperately wanted him to be my cheerleader and supporter. I wanted, I needed, his approval and blessing. I needed him to reassure me that I was doing the right thing, and, most important, to tell me I was capable. Instead, he said a quick goodbye, and I got in my car and left.

I headed out of our neighborhood and toward the highway. My old self wanted to go back and apologize, return the car, and make everyone happy. This was how I'd usually managed conflict. I would concede and try to be a better person. But now I could not go back. More importantly, I would not. I had to keep going toward my destination.

My mom was thrilled to take this trip. Like me, she had lived in my father's shadow and had never realized her life-long dreams. Trips like this were an opportunity to be herself. Having her with me was a relief. Though she was not sure what to think of my dreams and my experiences, she was game to travel with me. We got along well, and I knew I would have a fun traveling companion to keep me company and make me feel safe. Curiously, while my mother did little to pursue her dreams, she was confident in my abilities to achieve mine. No matter what I was doing, she would tell me, "You can do it. I know you can."

The new-car smell reminded me of my boldness during the past days. I was traveling to Montrose to visit the Ute Indian Museum and see Chipeta's homestead. I hardly recognized myself.

Chapter Seven
Coming Home

The morning of our departure for Montrose, Mom and I put our luggage in the trunk of my car, and a thermos of hot coffee in the front seat with us. Under the cover of darkness, my mom and I drove west on Highway 50 toward Montrose. I shivered from the crisp, frigid air. I took a deep breath. *This is crazy*, I thought. *How far will I go to write Chipeta's story?*

I felt different. Was it apprehension about my boldness? No, it was something other than that. I had turned forty-four that January and was beginning to claim my life's journey. What I felt was empowerment. I wanted to grow up and face my own life; I wanted to give my children the opportunity to do the same. I had smothered them with what I thought was motherly love but had really operated from a place of fear. I would not have been able to bear it if something happened to them. I was also afraid they would not live up to their grandparents' expectations. I worried what would happen to me if I did not have the children close to me. They were my reason to stay put. Keeping myself involved in their lives held me back from moving forward in my own life. The older my kids got, the harder it was to control them. During this time, a dear friend said, "I know you love your children, but you must let them grow up. You need to let them be independent." She was right. Only I still needed an excuse to avoid living my own authentic life.

I had consulted a gifted psychic, Maria, who was also my massage therapist. She seemed to really listen as I told her about the dream and my journey. I was afraid that Mark and my family would ridicule me for visiting her, so I said nothing to them about it. My religious training forbade me from working with the "likes of her". Friends and family considered psychics and people who called themselves as an "intuitive" quacks or delvers into the paranormal. When I needed to talk to someone who could understand my past months, I went to Maria. She said that this journey was important for my growth. She reminded me that I had a direct tie to Chipeta and that this was part of my soul's voyage. There was a purpose for all I was experiencing, and the things I was supposed to learn would later reveal themselves to me.

I thought about the celestial beings at my bedside the previous morning. In my teens, when I lived in an old house in Cañon City, Colorado, I had visitations from a male spirit. When I told my parents about him, my father asked if I was on drugs. Later, my twin and I saw this spirit at the same time. It visited my older sister too. He was young and gaunt. He smiled at us. There was something in his demeanor that scared us silly. After that I would pray hard for protection and sleep with the light on.

I had sensed things about people and places before when I was a teenager and would later learn that what I had sensed had come to be. I would call them coincidences and push them aside. According to Catholic and Methodist doctrine, supernatural explanations for events are dangerous. This also meant I should not mess around with psychics, mystics, and any other spiritual practices not related to Christianity. Just before I left for Montrose, a trusted friend ominously warned me to, "Be careful that someone doesn't get you involved in a cult."

While the world still slept, my mother and I drove west through the small towns of Florence and Cañon City. I had never driven this route by myself and should have been anxious, but I was not. I felt relieved I was away from home and on the way to Montrose. We made our way through the dark and curvy canyons cradling the Arkansas River—once part of a vast ocean billions of years before Colorado's birth, and at another time where dinosaurs thundered across the landscape. I felt deep in my soul the history all around me. These canyons held the bones of Ute Ancestors who had lived in this region hundreds of years before easterners arrived.

Every now and then, I would feel a twinge of guilt for leaving Mark and the kids at home, for buying the new car, ignoring my mother-in-law's concerns, and for brushing past my husband's worry about my obsession with Chipeta. I would remind myself I needed this experience.

For miles on end, my mother and I said little. We watched in wonder as the sunlight caressed the rims of the steep canyons, bathing them in gold and orange light. As steam rose from the icy river the water looked like liquid gold and silver. We watched an angler devoutly trek down to the river's edge, hoping to catch hungry trout. It was a glorious morning, a new day filled with possibility.

We stopped for coffee in Salida, where I could only make small talk with my mother, as I was feeling another round of nervousness. I was about to drive over Monarch Pass. I had little experience with mountain driving, even though I was born and raised in Colorado. I had braved Berthoud Pass and minor passes near Nederland and the I-70 corridor, but I always left the other passes to Mark, because he did the tough mountain driving. This would be only my second time driving across the Continental Divide, which I had heard it could be treacherous.

After our break, we drove through Salida and continued west on Highway 50. Familiar landmarks reminded me of my childhood trips into the nearby canyons. As I mentioned earlier, my father, a writer, always shared a history lesson or two about the regions we were traveling through. He painted romantic images of the past, about Ute camps and the gold miners, who left scars on the land

and abandoned mineshafts and ghost towns all over the Rocky Mountains. I relished every word he said, because I could see the history and feel it inside me. He talked about peaceful settings with teepees camped beside creeks in grassy meadows, but he never shared the stark truth about what happened when miners and pioneers invaded Colorado territory by the thousands and how the United States government drove the Ute from Colorado. I wondered what the tribes thought about the invaders cutting down all their trees to build mine shacks and shafts and other structures, about people crawling across the land, digging into, and dynamiting the earth.

Just to the east of Monarch Pass stood the remains of the abandoned Madonna Mine, which once furnished lead, zinc, and silver to the steel industry. Not once while growing up did I learn about the ramifications of the Gold Rush and what they would mean for the Ute and other tribes. I was ignorant about this part of our history. What I had learned about Indigenous cultures came from Hollywood Westerns and, as I have said, outdated history books, and my father's stories.

The snow-capped Collegiate Mountains surrounded us now. Here the Ute had dragged travois—platforms or netting mounted on two long poles tied together in the shape of an elongated isosceles triangle to create a frame—across the rugged landscapes to their summer grounds in the east or west. The Ute observed nature and followed its seasons. When the animals migrated, so did the Ute. The mountains provided plentiful resources during the summer months: wild game and more than three hundred varieties of plants.

My mother and I slowly climbed the steep mountain pass toward the timberline. I looked ahead and inhaled deeply. *You can do this,* I thought. I gripped the steering wheel with my damp palms, while, in a firm voice, my mother coaxed me up the narrow highway. She told me about her father, a Norwegian logger, who had taught her to drive on narrow, steep roads in Wisconsin. "Follow the white line on the right," she said, her voice confident and encouraging, "and hug it a bit. Not too close." I did as she instructed, and I felt like a stranger had taken over my body. Who was the woman with the death grip on the steering wheel?

My mother had always been my rock. Out of necessity, by age thirteen she had already learned to cook, clean, be resourceful with leftover food, to sew or alter clothing, how to manage a household budget, and how to take care of a big family. Her mother, Mellie, taught her these skills, and Mellie's Norwegian mother and grandmother taught her. I had always looked up to my mother (I still do). I depended upon her to teach me how to be a good wife and mother. When I was twelve, she taught me how to take care of my baby sister, and later she encouraged me to babysit to earn money. She was brave. She had experienced major hardships, yet she always found a way to bounce back from them.

Snowdrifts covered in soot from exhaust and red and brown roadway dust stood six to eight-feet high. Rocks of varied sizes lay on the highway where they had fallen as the sun warmed the canyon walls, a reminder that snowstorms were prevalent in late April and that nature was unpredictable. Luckily for us, we avoided the rocks, and the roads were clear of ice and snow. With my mother's encouragement, I slowly and steadily drove westward. I silently wondered if we would ever get to the top of the pass.

Suddenly, at 11,312 feet, Monarch Pass appeared in all its breathtaking beauty. This majestic pass was part of the Sawatch Range in the Rocky Mountains, located in south-central Colorado. In 1880, business owners and miners built the crude, unpaved road making it possible for wagons and stagecoaches to travel across the Great Divide, thereby connecting the east and its booming mining camps with the west and towns like Gunnison, Colorado. This made it possible to sell and deliver goods to those living in the mining towns and camps. At the same time the United States government continued their relentless drive to force the Ute people out of Colorado and onto reservations. The world as Chipeta and her people knew it had changed beyond recognition.

At the top of the pass, I could scarcely believe what I saw: thousands upon thousands of towering, evergreens and huge aspen groves covered the rocky and snow-covered hillsides. Those the sun highlighted glowed while others nestled in the purple and blue shadows of morning. To my right, the steep slopes reached up toward an unseen sky. I could not even see the tops of them. To my left stood a massive ski lodge and chair lifts. It felt strange to see such a big building and parking lot at the top of a wild and rugged mountain.

When I looked forward and to my left, my legs turned to jelly. The sides of the mountain seemed to drop off into oblivion, into valleys with bottoms you could not see from the road. I was glad I was driving next to the canyon walls and not on the outer edge of the highway. I could hardly look at the sides of the mountains, as their height dwarfed everything around them, including the car. From an early age, I knew this place was the "Land of the Shining Mountains," a name used by the Ute people to describe the snowcapped peaks of the Colorado Rockies.

During late summer and early autumn, the Ute were known to travel by foot and horseback across the Divide and onto the eastern slopes of the Rocky Mountains and onto the eastern plains of Colorado. There they hunted buffalo, which sustained them through the long winter months. In the winter they made their way to lower elevations, where they set up camps near Conejos, Ignacio, Cortez, and other parts of the southwest. I recalled a WPA account about a bitter winter in the late 1860s. The Ute had traveled to Colorado Springs, then a small city built during the Gold Rush. They had gone there to ask the citizens for food, as the promised government rations had not arrived or had arrived spoiled, or insect infested. I imagined seeing the Ute was a memorable event for the pioneers living there.

The view from the top of Monarch Pass was spectacular and, I had to admit, it was equally spectacular on the other side of the pass. Each curve and switchback brought us face to face with nature's beauty. The forests of evergreens reminded me of soft velvet robes draped across the valleys. Massive granite boulders jutted from the tops of nearby hills; their chalky gray forms seemed to disappear into the clouds.

The roadway looked too steep. My mother suggested I shift my car into low gear. Grateful she was with me; I took deep breaths and did as she suggested. I could not talk, as I felt panicky and just needed to keep going. I wanted down, right then! It is an understatement to say I felt immense relief and joy when I finally reached the bottom of Monarch Pass.

Miles and miles of grass, scrub oak, and towering pines covered the steep slopes and filled the valleys stretched before us. The Gunnison River flowed down the mountains we had just crossed and spilled into greening meadows and through groves of aspen and cottonwoods. Spring runoff would not start for two months, and yet the river had already overflowed its mossy banks. Magpies bobbed up and down on fence posts and power lines, and a hawk circled high above. I cannot explain it, but I felt euphoric. I had a powerful urge to get out of the car and run across the land. I intimately knew this place. It was as though I was part of the land. I had the strangest sensation that if I stepped barefoot onto the grassy slopes and meadows, I would remember. *Remember what?*

Still driving, I opened the car windows and let the cold, crisp spring air in. The scents of sweet sage, spring willows, and damp earth filled the car. I inhaled deeply.

My soul had longed for this elixir. We reached Cochetopa Pass. A light dusting of snow covered the hillsides. A vibrant, blue sky kept vigil over them. This scene brought into sharper focus the history I had read about Chipeta and Ouray, when they lived at the first Los Piños agency.

In 1861, shortly after tens of thousands of miners began arriving in Ute territories, the Ute met with United States government officials to discuss and eventually sign the Conejos Treaty. The Ute hoped to avoid conflicts with the miners and settlers. This treaty limited the Ute to approximately 23.5 million acres west of the Continental Divide. The government promised to keep easterners out of the Ute territories, where Chipeta and her people hoped to live in peace.

The greedy silver and gold miners regularly trespassed on the new Ute territories. These miners complained to the government that they should have access to this land, and soon the Ute faced another treaty negotiation. On March 2, 1868, Ute leaders signed the Hunt Treaty, which stated that the western third of the region would be set aside for the Ute. This became the first Los Piños Agency, located near the Los Piños River. After this, the government moved the Ute from agency to agency until their lands dwindled to little more than fifteen million acres. There was nothing the Ute could do to stop the migration of miners and others who followed them there. It created havoc on the lands, destroying the very resources the Ute depended upon for food and medicine.

Scores of cream-colored sheep grazed peacefully along the highway, oblivious to our presence. Their wooly coats muted the clank of their bells. Chipeta and Ouray were skilled sheepherders. As young boys, Ouray and his brother once worked for sheep ranchers in the region we now call Taos, New Mexico. There they learned to raise and herd sheep. They learned to speak Spanish, a skill that would help them during negotiations with the government and other tribes in the region. Chipeta also learned how to raise sheep and speak Spanish.

Ongoing migration of the outsiders eventually led to the Ute signing the Brunot Treaty on September 13, 1873. This meant that the Tabeguache Ute people would move to the new Los Piños II Agency, located along the Uncompahgre River, near what is now known as Montrose.

The government moved other Ute bands to reservations in eastern Utah and southwest Colorado, near present-day Ignacio and Cortez. Chipeta and Ouray planned to live out their lives on their allotted lands according to the treaty. But sadly, the United States government had other plans.

Chapter Eight

Meeting of Hearts and Minds

Chipeta and her brother, John McCook are buried side-by-side on the grounds of Ouray Memorial Park, in Montrose. 2002.

I stood at the foot of Chipeta's tomb. Seeing her name engraved in the concrete structure made my grief overwhelming. My tears poured. She had experienced so many losses throughout her life: she and Ouray had lost their son, Pahlone and the United States government had repeatedly moved the tribes from one location to another. After Ouray's death in 1880, the government had taken their allotted land. According to the government officials, Indigenous women were not allowed to own property. Soon the homestead and many of the furnishings were auctioned off.

Chipeta was born in 1843, when trappers and traders were making their way into the region. There is no doubt she witnessed first-hand the relentless appetite of the United States government, miners, and traders, who had come to harvest the resources of Ute territories. Early in our country's history, when the Europeans landed on the east coast of America, they believed they were part of "manifest destiny," a belief that God meant for the newly arrived immigrants to rule the land and its resources. This belief spread like wildfire across the country.

This was one of the reasons, out of many, why the government moved the Ute from one government agency to another. One move was to the area now called Montrose. I stood where Chipeta and Ouray once farmed. They transformed this once barren landscape into a fine farm. They built their adobe home near the Uncompahgre River, and successfully raised sheep, horses, and crops.

Looking around at the beauty of the cottonwood trees, the lush meadows, the river, I could not imagine how awful it was for Chipeta to see her life disintegrate like it did. "I am here, Chipeta," were the only words I could muster. With blurry vision and tear-filled eyes, I stumbled to the wrought iron fence that wrapped around Chipeta's tomb and her brother's grave and held on to it with both hands. A powerful energy surged from the earth and spread to the surrounding area. Even the trees, bushes, and graves seemed animated. I could feel the vibration of this energy move into the bottoms of my feet and through my entire being. In this state, I felt connected to everything around me. I sensed that if I had lain on the ground, the earth would have swallowed me up. What was happening was incomprehensible.

My mother got out of the car and joined me at the tomb. Of course, I could not tell her what had just happened. What would she have thought? I did not know for sure what *I thought*. I turned toward the museum and saw CJ walking toward me. She had long black hair that almost reached her waist, and a smile I will never forget. "Sister!" she called out. When she reached me, we embraced, and once again I cried.

CJ told me she was Oglala Lakota Sioux, from the Pine Ridge Reservation in South Dakota. I introduced her to my mother and we three stood in front of Chipeta's tomb and talked about the Ute Indian Museum and the surroundings. Next, Mom and I followed CJ into the museum. I stepped from my world into the past. Piñon and sage incense filled the air with smoky sweetness. A wooden flute played a haunting melody while hide drums echoed the tempo. The rasping sounds of moraches, notched-wooden percussion instruments, sounded through the interior of the museum as a video of the Ute Bear Dance played for visitors.

As I made my way through the exhibition halls, I felt like I was floating. The similar energy I felt at the tomb seem to surround me when I paused in front of the various artifacts and photographic images. I saw personal belongings from Chipeta and Ouray's early days alongside the Uncompahgre River.

I looked at a photo of Chipeta taken in her early life in 1873. It was a familiar one I had seen during my research trip to the History Colorado Center library. Same as before, her beautiful features mesmerized me. Chipeta had an amazing presence. Searching her face, I saw determination and poise. I saw strength, too.

Chipeta sat on the ground next to her husband, Ouray, and a host of Ute and United States government delegates. The photo captured a crucial time in Ute history following the Brunot Treaty talks. The Ute signed away their rights to their government allotted lands at the first Los Piños Agency and would move to the Los Piños II agency.

Felix Brunot used the loss of Chipeta and Ouray's son Pahlone to encourage Ouray to sign the treaty. Pahlone (also called Paron), almost five, had proven himself a capable rider after he had climbed onto Ouray's prized war horse, Thunder Cloud. Men in the tribe had tried to ride this horse to no avail. Thunder Cloud ran and Pahlone held on for dear life. The horse ran toward a gnarly tree and knocked Pahlone off its back, wounding Pahlone's shoulder. This wound became a symbol of his bravery. This meant he could accompany the next hunting party to the eastern plains of Colorado to hunt for bison.

Members of the Arapaho tribe raided the hunting camp which was located somewhere near present day Fort Morgan. A skirmish between the two tribes ensued. During the battle, Pahlone was taken captive. Ouray and Chipeta searched in vain for their son but could not find him. It must have been excruciating to return home without him.

Felix Brunot had befriended Ouray, and later told the heartbroken couple if Ute leaders signed the Brunot Treaty the United States government would help them reunite with their son. In 1873, the Brunot Treaty between the Ute and the United States government was signed in good faith. Sadly, Pahlone never came home. Brunot brought an Arapaho boy about Pahlone's age to Ouray and Chipeta, but the boy said he hated the Ute. Ouray declared that the boy was not his. What sorrow the couple must have felt. I wondered how Brunot could have been so cruel and conniving. Accounts in historical archives said that Chipeta and Ouray were distraught and never got over the loss of their son.

Another display case held a well-worn dress made by Chipeta. I felt her presence as I studied its tiny form. She had been petite, compared to me. It was an aged, black wool dress that she had altered. I could see the tiny stitches she had made in the fabric. I smiled because she, like most women, had experienced changes in her body. She had gained weight and needed to let her dress out a bit. Next to her dress lay a beautiful, beaded buckskin doll and an amazing toy cradleboard she had made in her later years. Everywhere I looked, I saw remnants from her early life and that of the Ute people.

In still another display case, there was a robe belonging to Chief Ignacio, headdresses, and Ouray's buckskin shirt, made and finely beaded by Chipeta. He too was small of stature. Chipeta had tied medicine bundles to the front of it, to heal his illness and ward off evil.

After Mom and I had toured the museum, CJ told me that Roland's schedule had suddenly cleared, and he would indeed be coming to the museum the following evening. He was to speak at a potluck dinner hosted by the Friends of the Ute. They invited us to participate in the event and to meet Roland, Chipeta's *great, great grandson.* I could hardly believe it.

By now, Valorie was somewhere between Utah and Montrose. She would join us for the dinner at the museum on Saturday. CJ suggested that my mother and I visit the Council Tree in Delta, Colorado, a half-hour's drive north, while we waited for Valorie. We thought it was a promising idea, so we got in the car and drove toward the sleepy town of Delta.

As we drove, the landscape took on a whole new meaning for me. This was not just a land of sagebrush and yucca, or of chalky white bluffs, but was traditional homelands of the Ute. It was where Chipeta once lived and her where her tomb remained. The landscape felt personal. I choked back tears as I recalled the large photo mural in the Chipeta Room of the museum. Pictured were the Ute crossing the Grand River (now called the Colorado River) and slogging toward their uncertain future.

Chapter Nine
Delta Council Tree

I have always loved trees. As a child I loved nothing better than to climb to their branches high off the ground and sit in the canopy of leaves. I would feel the trees were wise old spirits who watched over me while I played. To me, they were living beings with heartbeats. Even today, when my husband and I need to sever a branch from a tree, I feel sad, and I wonder if the tree feels the pain of letting go.

When I was a child in Colorado Springs, there was a large willow tree in the Smith's yard, just south of our yard. The Smith boys built a wooden treehouse in its lower branches, and my siblings and I loved to climb into this amazing hideaway. When the Smiths were not in the yard, I would climb up there and sit all by myself. I loved my connection to the tree, and to the wind when it blew branches back and forth. I heard songs in the wind, and I would sing at the top of my lungs, feeling like I was part of the tree. Given this, I could not wait to see the historic Delta Council Tree.

I turned off Main Street in Delta and toward a quiet residential area surrounded by small houses and narrow graveled streets. And then there it was! I could not believe what I saw: a massive cottonwood reaching high into the morning sky. At eighty-five feet, it looked out of place, dwarfing the historical marker next to it, the houses, and the other mature trees in the area. I quickly parked the car, and my mother and I rushed to it.

***Mom and I stood in awe at the Delta Council Tree's massive size!* 2002.**

We stood below the tree's ancient canopy and peered up and up through layers of gnarly branches. Spring winds were blowing hard and making the enormous tree branches creak and groan while they bobbed up and down. Its trunk was more than seven feet in diameter. My mother and I hugged it and tried to wrap our arms around it and grasp each other's hands. It was impossible. The trunk held dark scars and deep, mysterious caverns where large branches once held fast. These recesses felt like doorways to another time and place. We were two children moving around the tree and marveling at the weathered grays and sandy browns of its bark. I felt its tremendous energy.

The historical marker presented by the local Daughters of the American Revolution, said the tree is a Colorado landmark, dedicated to the memory of Chief Ouray, his wife, Chipeta, and all the Ute tribes. It said Ute and non-Indigenous people had met under its branches to smoke the peace pipe and to settle cultural differences. It was more than two hundred years old. Chipeta and Ouray had not even been born when it sprouted into being. I thought about the Ute's history and all the changes that took place in the region over those two hundred years. Despite harsh weather and western expansion, the tree had withstood the winds of change. So, too, did the Ute.

I rested my hand on the tree trunk and closed my eyes. I grasped that my life and my body were like this tree. Parts of me were missing. I had been through unbearable losses, hardships, and physical illnesses, and yet, like this ancient tree, I was still standing, resilient and hopeful. I offered a prayer of gratitude for my safe arrival in Montrose and for the experiences that were to come. I prayed for Chipeta and the Ute people—past, present, and future. Once again, energy filled my body, moving from the ground up, as it had at Chipeta's tomb. I felt alive and at home.

***Delta Council Tree.* Artwork by Vickie Leigh Krudwig. 2006**

My eyes still closed, the wind shifted, as spring winds often do, and suddenly the pungent scent of tobacco smoke permeated the air. Its rich, earthy aroma enveloped the tree, my mother, and me. I opened my eyes and was surprised to see there was no one near us. There was not a logical explanation for this phenomenon. Puzzled, my mother and I looked at each other. Deep down inside, I knew the smoke was from another source, one that defied reason, a spiritual source. I shivered, knowing the Ute held councils there; no doubt, participants smoked tobacco then. Was this an acknowledgement of my presence?

Prior to going to Delta, my spiritual awareness of the world around me had been expanding bit by tiny bit. I had realized there was more to the spiritual world than I had known. I had secretly explored various kinds of spirituality, and now I was learning about Indigenous spirituality. While I cherished my Catholic and Methodist traditions, I was now finding beauty in the reverence the Indigenous demonstrated for the living Earth and all its living things. In the last year, and even in the last day, I had experienced dreams, visitations, CJ's understanding, the Ute Indian Museum, and now the power and energy of the Delta Council Tree. My soul opened wide. I was ready to receive whatever it was I was going to learn.

Years before this journey, Mark, the kids, and I had driven through the Wind River Reservation in Wyoming on our way to Yellowstone National Park. I had known nothing about reservations. We stopped at a gift shop near the reservation, and there I bought a cassette tape featuring flute music of Carlos Nakai. I loved his music. I resonated with it. I would play it in the car or in my studio while I created art or authored stories. The more I would listen, the more I explored other Indigenous artists. The melodies and the voices of the performers transfixed me. I played this type of music throughout my *Searching for Chipeta* book project, and now while painting in my art studio.

In 2004, after *Searching for Chipeta* came out, my husband told me about an Indigenous radio station, Alter-Native Voices, a weekly program hosted by Suzie Aikman, a member of the Eastern Band Cherokee. Suzie highlighted Indigenous musicians and authors and helped keep the culture alive and well. She also introduced people like me to the world of Indigenous arts. Mark encouraged me to reach out to Suzie, and I did. Eventually, my son and I volunteered there as production assistants. During our stint there, we had the privilege of meeting many talented Indigenous musicians and learning about their cultures and beliefs.

I started going to the Denver March Powwow, where I was thrilled by the sight of hundreds of Indigenous groups dressed in their traditional regalia. Young and old celebrated their cultural connections to the past. They danced in the arena, accompanied by drummers and singers. It gave me chills, and I knew, without a doubt, the Ancestors were present and dancing with their descendants.

When the audience was to invited join in, I hesitantly left the grandstand and stepped into the arena, and I danced shoulder to shoulder with people from diverse cultures and tribes. We moved as one around the great arena, and I knew we were all connected. For an instant, I belonged to something holy and meaningful. I had desperately wanted to belong to this culture, I had longed for it, yet I was keenly aware that I was not part of this history, and I never would be. Years later, when I collaborated with Ute men and women and with other Indigenous groups, I would feel out of place and awkward. Aware of this, I still strove to learn all I could from them through their words, music, art, and dance. The more I learned the more alive I felt inside.

Even after I had finished writing Chipeta's story, I listened to the music. Whenever I heard Indigenous flutes and drums, my mind traveled to Chipeta's time and that of her People. These sounds, along with jingle dancers, often transported me back to my childhood and early experiences of learning about the Ute people and watching them dance in Manitou Springs, just west of Colorado Springs. The jingles on the dancers' dresses were sometimes made of metal lids from tobacco cans. The flattened lid would be rolled into a cone shape and sewn onto their dresses. When the women danced the metal lids made a sound like jingle bells.

We had a cabin in the woods in Chalk Creek Canyon near Nathrop, a small town west of Buena Vista. We would drive through Manitou Springs and up Highway 24, which once had been the old Ute trail. Once at our cabin, we would spend hours hiking and looking for arrowheads. We knew how to spot flint, arrowheads, and scrapers. My father used to tell me I had an eye for finding them. With great delight I soaked up these moments. I also enjoyed being by myself in the groves of aspen beneath the cliffs across from our cabin. I would talk, sing, and play loudly, just in case the Ute Ancestors were watching. Now, standing at the base of the Delta Council Tree, I re-experienced that spiritual presence of the Ute. It was such a warm and loving embrace.

Chapter Ten

Meeting Chipeta's Descendant

After our trip to see the Delta Council Tree, Mom and I met Valorie at the Holiday Inn Express in Montrose, just a mile or so from the Ute Indian Museum. We only had an hour before we needed to return to the museum, so Mom and I hurriedly exchanged greetings with Valorie and tried to tell her what had just happened at the Delta Council Tree.

Once we were back at the museum, CJ greeted us at the door and informed us Roland McCook would speak at the dinner that night. He would talk about the Meeker Incident and how it changed history for his Ancestors and future generations. It was exactly two years to the day since I had had the first dream about Chipeta. To say I was nervous about meeting Roland, would be an understatement. Everything taking place felt surreal.

When Roland and I first talked over the phone in October 2000, he had seemed uninterested in what I had to say, almost hostile. But then, once I had told him about the dream, his demeanor changed, and his voice was kinder. He validated my dreams and my role as a writer who could tell Chipeta's story. CJ introduced me to the guests as they filed into the meeting room. They were members of the Friends of the Ute, community members, museum staff, and others. We all filled our plates at the buffet and waited for our featured guest to arrive.

I was about to take my first bite when Roland walked into the room. He was handsome, dressed in crisply pressed blue jeans, a black western shirt, and polished black cowboy boots. He had tied his long black hair, streaked with whisps of gray, in a ponytail. His gaze was intense, and I watched as his dark eyes scanned the room. CJ walked over to Roland and greeted him. She motioned me over and introduced me. Roland and I shook hands but said little. I felt as though I had never spoken to him before. His expression was unreadable, and he did not seem interested in socializing with me. Trembling and doubtful, I quickly joined my mother and Valorie, who sat at a nearby table. My heart was pounding and I could hardly taste my food.

Roland walked over to a large sliding glass door, which framed a stunning view of the snowcapped San Juan Mountains. The sun was beginning to set, its rays illuminating the trees and rounded bales of hay behind the museum. Charcoal gray clouds streaked with purples and blues gathered. Large trees whipped up and down in the wind. It was as if they were acknowledging Roland's presence. The room became quiet, and he began speaking in a soft, eloquent voice. Spellbound, I listened to him talk about his Ute family and his long-gone Ancestors. As he described the Ute way of life before the trappers, traders, miners, and the United States cavalry came into their territories, his voice took on a sorrowful tone as he described the last free days of the Ute, Chipeta, and Ouray.

Times were changing in ways they could not have imagined. They tried but failed to dam the flow of non-Indigenous people into their territories. He described the promises the United States government made to Ute leaders, how the people were eager to keep the peace with the newcomers and soldiers. The Ute had signed at least five treaties granting them rights to territories, but the newcomers and the United States government always found reasons to break the treaties and take the land. The Ute had to move from one Indigenous agency to another. Shortly after signing the Brunot Treaty, the Tabeguache were moved again, this time to the area now called

Montrose. The White River Ute settled near the area that is now called Meeker, Colorado.

Roland told us United States government officials had encouraged the Ute to try their hand at farming. So, Ouray and Chipeta worked hard to please these officials and to keep the peace. They wanted to demonstrate that the Ute could change with the times.

Then Roland paused. The room was silent. And all eyes were on him. He said Chipeta, Ouray, and their adopted children cleared the land and dug irrigation ditches that stretched across their property. They cultivated hay for their livestock and planted gardens. Within a brief time, they had established an impressive farm, complete with an adobe home filled with furnishings familiar to non-Indigenous people. They made sure their door was always open to the government officials and visitors.

With a pained expression, Roland told us that the couple's efforts to befriend the newcomers were successful. But they did not placate settlers encroaching on the new Los Piños II agency lands. Envious that the Ute had fine things and well-run farms, newcomers complained that the Ute were taking food out of their children's mouths. They demanded that the United States government rid Colorado of the Ute, for the last time.

In the summer of 1879, the Meeker Incident at the White River Agency sealed the Ute's fate. Indian Agent Nathan Meeker told the Ute they had to plow and plant their meadows. But these meadows provided grass for their prized ponies and food and shelter for the people. The Ute were hunters and gatherers. They had no desire to destroy their lands. Meeker, impatient, and unwilling to listen to the Ute's concerns, started plowing a meadow himself. Ute men confronted him about this, there was an argument, and a Ute man pushed him. Afraid for his life, Meeker asked the government for help, and the authorities sent soldiers to his aid.

General George Crook ordered Major Thomas T. Thornburgh, 191 officers, soldiers, and civilians to assist Meeker at the White River Agency. Thornburgh and his entourage would be trespassing on Ute lands set aside for them by the United States government through a treaty in 1868. Fearful there would be a massacre like the Sand Creek Massacre of 1864, the Ute warned Thornburgh not to trespass on reservation lands. Leading up to the Sand Creek Massacre, soldiers ignored the rights and boundaries of the Cheyenne and Arapaho and trespassed onto their reservation. Then in a predawn surprise attack, they slaughtered hundreds of men, women, and children.

Site of the Meeker Agency near Meeker, Colorado. 2005.

Ignoring the Ute's warnings, Major Thornburgh and his soldiers refused to turn back and planned to invade the reservation. To cross Milk Creek meant soldiers were breaking the treaty of 1868. Still Thornburgh and his troops were undaunted. They made their advance and Ute warriors quickly attacked the men. Thornburgh died. Some of Thornburgh's men had died too. Captain J. Scott Payne, filling in for Thornburgh, instantly sent messengers for help. Soon the Ninth Cavalry, a Black regiment of 450 men, led by Colonel Wesley Merritt was enroute to assist Thornburgh's remaining men. Another battle loomed. For six days Thornburgh's surviving troops fought to hold their positions until help arrived. At the end of the conflict seventeen men were dead and forty-four had been wounded.

The White River Agency conflict had become deadly as well. Nathan Meeker and ten others from the White River Agency were dead. Ute warriors had taken Meeker's wife and daughter, plus another woman and her two young children hostage.

Meanwhile, a messenger alerted Chipeta about the conflict. Ouray was hunting at the time, so Chipeta sent a runner to relay the news to him. He instantly sent a message to the White River Ute, telling them not to fight agency employees or officials. Then he rallied other Ute leaders to help rescue the Meeker hostages, but before they could put any plan into action, the captors released the women and children, who then traveled to Chipeta and Ouray's home, where Chipeta treated them kindly. She cried tears of compassion and dread when she heard about what had happened. Ouray shed his white man's clothes and, from then on, wore his traditional buckskin.

News of the Meeker Incident spread across the country. "The Utes Must Go" became a slogan much repeated by the national press, and Colorado newspapers spread panic and fear by lying about the Ute. They blamed wildfires on the Ute. They declared that the Ute were burning everything in their path. Tensions were high.

The saddest part of this story was that the government officials used words such as "exterminate" and "obliterate" when they talked about what they wanted done with the Ute still living in Colorado. The words left me icy cold and shivering. These were human beings, Ute Ancestors, the government was talking about.

In January 1880, Ute leaders, including Ouray, went to Washington, D.C. for a hearing about the Meeker Incident. Chipeta accompanied Ouray, as he was quite ill with Bright's Disease (kidney nephritis). Doctors had tried to heal his condition but had failed. He was dying. He and the other Ute leaders knew the government would force them to leave the Los Piños II agency. The Ute people faced an uncertain future.

In August 1880, Chipeta and Ouray, and other Ute leaders, made a trip to Ignacio to talk about another new treaty—one that would completely change their lives. Ouray was disillusioned with the treaties and the United States government, and yet the government wanted the Ute to sign another one. This meant another move. Too many promises had already been broken and traditional Ute territories had diminished dramatically. Sadly, United States government officials continued to pressure Ouray to convince the others to sign the new treaty. But even on his deathbed, Ouray was reluctant to do so. Citizens and United States government officials eagerly waited for the outcome of the treaty, so they could rush the land.

Ouray died on August 24, 1880. I imagined Chipeta's wails of grief. Her beloved husband of twenty-one years was gone. She and trusted tribal members buried Ouray in a secret location along the Los Piños River, and then she eventually returned to her home. After this, the government took her home from her. At that time, the United States government did not allow Indigenous women to own property, so it auctioned off her property to the highest bidder. Her land, her home, and most of her belongings were no longer hers. Otto Mears, a Colorado railroad builder, and a Dutch immigrant purchased Chipeta and Ouray's homestead for a ridiculously low price. The United States government made Mears pay Chipeta $700 from the sale.

United States government officials once again manipulated the Ute. Officials told them they would move them to a new reservation near present-day Grand Junction, Colorado, with the caveat that if the land were inhospitable for farming, they would go instead to the Uintah-Ouray Reservation in northeastern Utah. Of course, the fertile land was deemed "inhospitable" by the United States officials.

By September 1881, the calvary rounded up the Ute bands from the various agencies and campsites in the Uncompahgre region. Armed soldiers forced the White River and Tabeguache Ute living in the region to make the long trek to the Uintah-Ouray Reservation in Utah.

Roland's presentation ended. No one in the room moved. I heard muffled crying. My eyes filled with tears, and I dabbed at them with a napkin. I was trying to hold in my emotions. I knew if I started crying, I would not be able to stop. Roland's pain for his Ancestors and descendants was real, and for the Ute people, and it showed in his expression. They had lost so much.

Following Roland's presentation, a local archeologist showed slides from excavations done ahead of a pipeline planned from Meeker, Colorado, into New Mexico. Along the projected route, pipe workers and archeologists unearthed Ute artifacts, including wickiups. He continued his passionless talk while I fought being sick to my stomach about people disturbing these sacred places.

As the program concluded, dark charcoal-colored storm clouds gathered over the mountains and shrouded the museum and the land it sat upon. A loud clap of thunder rattled the windows and shook the walls, and, as if on cue, it rained. I felt sorrow deep within me. When I finally had the chance to let go, my tears fell like the rain.

Chapter Eleven
A Blessing and a Burden

The next morning, Valorie, my mother, and I planned to caravan with Roland, CJ, and her kids up to Wiesbaden Hot Springs and Spa in Ouray, where I hoped Roland would bless my book project. Before then, Valorie, Mom, and I walked across the street to Chipeta Lake. Aside from trills of red-winged blackbirds, it was a quiet Sunday morning. The lake's surface was smooth as glass. Fingerling trout rose to the top of the water in search of a morning meal. Their strikes created circular ripples that expanded into the Four Sacred Directions. Five Canada geese flew overhead and across the Uncompahgre River, just a short walk from Lake Chipeta. I could see why Chipeta, and Ouray loved their farmstead so much.

We were reverent as we walked around the lake, as there was a heightened awareness of the magnitude of what we were walking through. Then we crossed back over the road and met Roland and CJ at the museum. They planned to give us a personal tour of the Uncompahgre region, traditional homelands of the Ute people. Roland was personable and kind this morning, and for that I was grateful. He told me to follow his vehicle and stop when he stopped, so he could show us important places.

As promised, Roland and CJ pulled to the side of the road, got out of their car, and pointed out buildings and areas important to the Ute: a fort, the first school, a meadow where the Ute kept their ponies. But then came the unexpected and breathtaking view of Ridgway, Colorado. It

The mountains near Ridgeway were spectacular. The Ute migrated to the mountains during the hot weather. Their ponies grazed in the lush meadows. 2002..

was spectacular! I felt like the mountains were familiar, that I knew them even though I had never seen them. Were they in my dream about Chipeta?

Ridgway was a small community nestled between a series of pristine red mountain ranges rising high and jagged against this morning's blue spring sky. The Uncompahgre River ambled through the land. The Ute had camped in the surrounding lush, grass covered meadows during the warm summer months. It was a welcome retreat after long winters in southern Colorado.

As we entered the town, I felt an ominous presence, and in my mind's eye it was 121 years earlier. I saw cavalry soldiers riding into the Ute camps and rounding up the men, women, and children for a passage to certain disaster. Young children looked questioningly at their parents, who packed up their teepees and prized possessions, knowing they may never see their beloved mountains again, where Sinawaf, the Creator, had created the people.

I pulled my car over and wept bitterly. I no longer was blind to the atrocities that Chipeta and her people had suffered. I wept for Roland and Chipeta's descendants, and for all Ute forebears who had lost so much. I could not stop crying, so Valorie traded places with me and drove the rest of the way to our destination. Whether we liked it or not, we now had a deeper understanding of the upheaval of the Ute way of life that had occurred after Ouray's death.

We arrived in Ouray mid-morning. The clear and clean air smelled of pine and sage. Red sandstone cliffs and jagged granite peaks covered in a layer of brilliant white snow, surrounded the town. While we stood in front of the Wiesbaden Hot Springs and Spa, Roland approached and asked me to follow him up a dirt road that ran just behind the spa. My heart pounded. Maybe it was the altitude. Was it the reality of what I had learned over the past few hours? As we walked up the slope, Roland turned and made a sweeping gesture with his right arm. "This could have been my home," he said.

Roland's words hit me hard. He, like many Utes, lived on the Uintah-Ouray Reservation in Utah. The Ute Mountain Ute, Southern Ute, and White Mesa Ute lived on reservations in southwestern Colorado, and southeastern Utah. Roland had been born on the Uintah-Ouray Reservation, as was his father and his father's father. We walked up the hill in silence. Trying to hold back my emotions, I gulped mountain air. But this was no use; my grief was too deep. I began to sob uncontrollably. I struggled to walk up the hill. "I'm so sorry," I said, as we reached the top. Roland reached out his hand in a gesture of friendship. I put my hand in his.

Roland and I sat down on the ground three yards away from the front porch of a tiny white house. Though it was mid-April, and snow still covered parts of the hillsides, the heat from the vapor caves below us warmed the ground. Roland told me that Chipeta and Ouray's summer home was once here. This house had long ago replaced their original adobe home. Roland pointed to the red cliffs and told me that Ouray had hunted mountain sheep there while Chipeta waited below. He told me he had taken only one other white person to this place, as it was sacred to him and the Ute people.

The caverns, now housed in the Wiesbaden structure, were also sacred to the Ute, who had made regular pilgrimages to the site. For centuries the Ute soaked in the hot mineral water and prayed. They also led their horses into the caves to be healed and blessed by the natural hot springs. Unable to look Roland in the eye, I stared at an ant crawling along the dirt pathway.

I listened carefully while Roland spoke of his Ancestors. Then we talked about my dream and about my desire to honor Chipeta's request to write her story. We sat quietly and after a moment Roland turned to me and said, "I will bless your book, but I have three things I want from you. One, respect Chipeta, my Ancestors, and my family; two, tell the truth as you write her story; and finally," he looked at me and added the third request, "respect yourself." The last request seemed weird to me, and yet I agreed. I would not understand the significance of that request until much later. After another pause, he softly said, "This book will be a blessing and a burden."

Without saying a word, we sat side by side. Then a bird called out. Its cry was otherworldly. Shivers ran up and down my spine. The morning was calm. The front door of the tiny house slowly squeaked open. We turned to it. Then Roland looked at me and gently said, "Chipeta is telling you welcome. She is opening her door to you."

"I am opening my heart," I said, "that I might have a clear understanding of Chipeta's life."

In silence, Roland and I walked back down the hill and joined the others. Our group registered at the front desk of the spa, picked up our towels, and headed into the lower level of the building. Within moments warm moist air from the vapor caves replaced the cool mountain air. We used the dressing rooms to change into our swimsuits, then walked through the first of three caves. It held warm water and an area of cool water running over a rock wall, and a line of benches. I felt anxious when we moved to the second cave, its entrance a heavy wooden door. It held a shallow pool fed by a trickle of warm water coming from the top of the cave. When we reached the third cave, Roland whispered to me, "You need to earn your blessing. Try to stay in as long as you can." I slowly stepped into a world unlike any I had ever experienced.

Heat and steam assaulted me, burned my nostrils and skin. It was stifling. A pool of naturally heated water nearly filled the cave. Benches cut out of rock lined one side. Feeling claustrophobic, Valorie turned back for the first cave. It took at least two minutes for my eyes to adjust to the dim light and overpowering heat. Only a single light bulb lit the space. There was no sound system. Water dripped through openings in the cave. I tried to imagine the Ute and their horses soaking in here.

I stood, feeling as though I were somebody else, while Roland gave us instructions. *Am I really here?* I had lost myself over the years and had no idea who I was or where I was going. Roland nudged me forward. I tentatively dipped my big toe in the water and winced. I did not know it would be this hot. It was scalding, and yet I stepped all the way into it and moved toward the center of the pool. I grimaced as I sat down. Sweat poured into my eyes. I had to earn my blessing, summon my courage, and stay in the water, no matter what.

Unexpectedly, I understood the significance of the moment. I was washing away my past, cleansing my heart and spirit of the pain I had carried, so I could receive the future. A sob rose from the pool and echoed on the cave walls. It was mine. I was releasing years of pain, grief, regret, anger, and self-doubt. In that moment I relinquished control and dedicated myself to Chipeta and the Ancestors and the project. I acknowledged that I was on a sacred journey about to change my life. I closed my eyes and prayed for help. I was afraid of changing who I was. I knew it would affect every aspect of my life, including my relationships.

As I soaked, I continued my prayers. I asked for protection and the ability to see this epic project through. *Give me courage* I pleaded. "Help me, Grandmother," I whispered. I turned to my right and opened my eyes. An old man's emaciated face with hollow and aged eyes appeared on the cave wall. Two eagle feathers hung down on the left side of his head. He was older than the Ancestors. I wondered if I was hallucinating because of the extreme heat. I slowly closed and opened my eyes. The face was still there. A deep moan filled the cavern. It echoed off the cave walls and turned into a low, slow song sung in a language I did not know. Perhaps the voice had come from someone in the other caves. I could not tell. It touched me deeply. I wanted to rationalize what I was hearing but could not. I wanted to make sense of everything that had happened since the dream. Why couldn't I just accept it all at face value? On the hill by the white house, Roland had said, "You think too much." I had a habit of analyzing everything—perhaps to validate myself and my decisions. And now I was sitting in an ancestral cave getting ready to take part in a story that would transform my life.

I closed my eyes and listened. When I finally opened them again, the song continued to echo off the rocky walls. Maybe someone was acknowledging my presence.

"I've never heard these voices before," said one of CJ's children, his eyes wide. "I'm getting out of here." Then all three children clamored out of the pool and into the other cave. The song continued. Astonished, Roland looked at CJ, my mother, and me.

Within minutes the chanting stopped. No one had to say anything. We knew we had experienced something extraordinary. Roland stood up and asked us to gather. CJ brought the children back into the cave while I went to Valorie and begged her to join us. I did not want her to miss this once-in-a-lifetime moment. She needed healing, like I did. She reluctantly agreed, and together we went back to the third cave, where Roland told us to stand and form a sacred circle. "Join hands," he said. My legs wobbled. The combination of heat, emotional release, and the blessing I was about to receive was too much for me.

I listened with gratitude as Roland offered a prayer in the ancient Ute language. It, too, echoed off the walls. His words seemed to move the water, which became illuminated and full of energy. One by one, he blessed each person in the circle. Then I heard Chipeta's and my name. I received my blessing. Now I could fulfill my promise to Chipeta. Connected to her in this place, I cried from happiness. I sensed her presence and, more importantly, her approval.

Weak and wrung out, I could hardly carry myself to the dressing room. My life's losses and anxieties up to this moment struck me hard—losing two babies early in pregnancy, the grief of my children leaving home, and fear of my own mortality, and of Mark leaving me. Things I could not talk about. I grieved my imperfections as a child, a daughter, a wife, and as a mother. I felt regretful that I had smothered my children. It made me sad I did not trust my intuitive and healing gifts. I had kept them hidden for years. I wanted to stay in the cave and avoid going home.

Still in my swimsuit, my towel wrapped around me, I sank down to the dressing room floor and wailed. I trembled because I had been taking tranquilizers for months for anxiety attacks. I was afraid of the future. I would have to take more journeys away from home. It would take time for this to sink in. I rested my forehead on my knees.

Thinking about this now, years later, I suspect I feared getting well. If I had overcome my anxiety and illnesses, I would want more out of life. Illness had kept me safe in some ways. I had limited myself to exploring a well-lived life, the life I really wanted. I desperately wanted healing. I wanted to stop my anxiety attacks and emergency room visits. The ancestor's song and Roland's blessing assured me healing would come. Unstoppable, my tears of happiness, sorrow, and regret flowed. The shield I had placed over my heart years ago had shattered into a million pieces. My soul was raw, wide open, and vulnerable.

"That is right, let it all out," a woman said in low soothing voice. She spoke with a thick accent I could not place. Was this the voice we heard in the cave? My forehead still resting on my knees, she sang a calming song in a language I did not recognize. I stopped shaking. Her song permeated my every pore and peace spread through me. I happened to look down. To my left I saw two bare brown feet. On one ankle was a beaded bracelet. I looked up to see the woman's face, but she was gone.

I changed into dry clothes and headed outside to the car. I could not, and would not, put my shoes on, as I knew the grounds of the Wiesbaden Hot Springs and Spa were sacred. I wanted to feel the earth under the soles of my feet. As I walked across the lawn, I realized I was walking in Chipeta's footsteps.

While I waited for everyone, I leaned against a tree trunk that had been part of a larger tree. I closed my eyes and inhaled. I was at peace, and I was grateful for this new beginning in my life. "You picked a good tree to lean on," said a woman, her voice familiar. "That is a very special place."

I opened my eyes. It was the woman who had been singing to me in the dressing room! She stood next to me. She wore a plain skirt and a light-colored blouse. She had shoulder length hair and an ageless and gentle face. Her brown eyes searched mine, and then she tipped her head toward the tiny white house I had walked to with Roland. "Somebody been up to the house?" she asked.

"Yes," I answered, aware that I was being tested.

"Who took you there?" she asked.

"Roland."

"Were words spoken?"

"Yes, a few," I said, not offering any details. I knew Roland's and my conversation had to stay between us for a while.

A smile spread across the woman's face. "You are a lucky woman," she said. She turned and started up the hill and toward the house. I stood up to thank her, but she vanished before I could.

Can things get any stranger? I asked myself, never imagining that writing Chipeta's book would lead to such amazing experiences.

When the group met back in the parking lot, we discussed going somewhere for lunch. I was too drained emotionally and physically to go and knew I needed time to decompress. I politely declined the invitation to lunch. We bid each other farewell and got into our vehicles. Grateful we had been part of a sacred and healing experience, Mom, Valorie, and I got into my car and started driving toward Montrose. We spent three-fourths of the drive quietly lost in our own thoughts. I gazed at the passing scenery and whispered prayers of gratitude.

Later that evening, CJ called us at the hotel and asked if we would meet her and Roland at the Ute Indian Museum. I had no idea what they wanted, but it did not matter. I was eager to see them again. We met them as the sun was getting ready to set. Though sunlight filtered through the cottonwood trees on the museum grounds, the air was chilly. CJ and Roland asked if I had felt anything when I walked beside the Uncompahgre River the prior morning.

My sister, Mom, and I had walked past the lake and down a narrow dirt trail. We passed into a grove of willow trees getting ready to bud out. The willows had intertwined at the top. The grass was soft and sweet smelling. I had the familiar sense of energy moving through my body. I imagined that if the raiders had not kidnapped Pahlone, he and his parents would have sat at the river's edge enjoying the quiet and beauty. As a child, I loved catching minnows or tadpoles when I played in creeks. I guessed Pahlone would have also loved doing this. I imagined the joy that Chipeta and Ouray would have had watching him grow up into manhood.

Spring Willows Alongside the Uncompahgre River. **Artwork by Vickie Leigh Krudwig.**

Walking by the Uncompahgre River with CJ and Roland now, I showed them where I had felt the energy, and they looked at one another and nodded. Then something pulled me to another area, where thick bushes full of spiderwebs grew by a ditch. I was afraid of spiders, but I pushed the webs away and walked down a trail. I found a pile of bear scat sitting on leaves. I picked up a stick and pushed the scat aside, and then… I felt it again. An energy so intense it made my legs weak. I brushed those leaves aside and uncovered perfectly placed white cobbles at the base of a small seep. *Was this a spring that Chipeta and Ouray had used?* It made sense; cobbles would have prevented mud from getting into their water baskets or buckets when they drew water into them. Why did I think this? I did not know. What led me to places like this? I could not say. Was I surprised? Nothing would have surprised me by then.

The sun set and Mom, Val and I returned to the hotel. It was time to think about going home. I had mixed feelings about it. One part of me felt I was already home. Attached to Montrose and Ouray, I felt like I had lived in these towns all my life. Another part of me longed to see my husband and children back in Denver. I was eager to share my weekend with them. I was also excited to get to work on Chipeta's story.

Chapter Twelve

The Long Road Home

After my trip, I felt torn between two worlds. Terribly homesick for Montrose and Ouray, I wanted to go back there. I could not get all the sights and sounds out of my mind, and I was mentally and physically restless. I felt like I had left part of my soul in the caves of Ouray and on the grounds of the Ute Indian Museum. And yet, the love of my life and my children in Denver were also my home.

I continued to attend church. I spoke little of my experiences to people outside my family. I tried to tell Mark about everything that had happened. He listened politely but did not say much beyond, "huh." I would keep talking, even though I was afraid he was doubting my sanity. His response was predictable, even though I wanted him to embrace and validate my weekend's experiences. He was supportive of the book project but could not get into the mystical experiences that came with it.

I would spend my early mornings journaling and praying. My views about religion in general were shifting. I would watch the sunrise and think of Chipeta and the Ute, on the eastern plains during buffalo hunts. I made small offerings of cornmeal and tobacco to The Four Directions and to Chipeta and her Ancestors. After Mark left for work and the kids left for school, I would perform a morning ritual of burning sage and sweet grass, blessings from the earth. It felt natural to do this, despite my Catholic and Methodist upbringing. Pulling the smoke from the sage and sweet grass over my face and body helped center me.

I wrote down what I saw and heard in my journals. I didn't want to forget the amazing experiences I was having.

The days flew by, and soon I was again completely preoccupied with research and stories about Chipeta and the Ute. Wherever I went, I sensed the history of the people and their situation after the miners and others came. I continued to have dreams, each one more vivid than the one before. I always wrote down what I saw and heard. Did they add to my homesickness for Montrose? I was not sure. Sometimes my longing to return made me ache inside. At one point, I asked Mark if he would be willing to move to there. Of course, he said no. It was illogical of me to think we could move there. He had his successful career with the State of Colorado and the kids had school. I knew I would just have to try to visit Montrose and Ouray as often as I could.

May 16, 2002

Grandmother, you walk in my heart and mind. I am filled with happiness and gratitude because you have welcomed me. I accept my responsibility to write your story and that of your people. May it open doors to healing and understanding.

Granddaughter, you struggle with sorrow still. Can you not understand that you are now part of me, part of Ouray's and my descendants? You are part of the Ute family—we are now connected on a spiritual plane—not just on a literary project. You are "homesick" for Montrose because your new family is there, and we are honored. You, too, now know the longing we held in our hearts as we struggled on the reservation. We, too, missed our farm and the valley. We were homesick. Now these things do not matter. The Ute people, these ancient Ancestors, are free once more and their spirits live on the lands that you live on ....

Trust in the Creator, as he is wise and will help you with all that you need. Be at peace, live fully today, and accept your gifts. We will travel this road to understanding together, and I will be with you as the journey continues....

With each new message came a heightened awareness and connection to everything and everyone in my presence. Even the natural world seemed clearer and more animated. I knew I must be observant of the world around me. My new kind of self-awareness sometimes made me feel out of place with my parents and siblings, and with certain groups of friends. Everything seemed different to me. I could say, I was refining my place in the world. I felt confident, strong, and determined to succeed in all areas of my life, including family relationships.

I threw myself back into running my greeting card business and writing Chipeta's book, while managing rapid changes taking place in my life and trying to keep things together at home. It was important to me to keep a tight schedule when it came to meals, laundry, household tasks, card orders, and business partner demands for more designs. I was exhausted, but I hated to say no.

Keeping everyone happy and on schedule gave me stability, or so I thought. Truth was, I felt like my life was still falling apart. Old negative patterns pushed aside my new and independent patterns and made me feel unsure of myself. There were times when I wanted to hide from the world. My anxiety disorder came back. Again, it seemed relentless.

Out of desperation, I decided to see my doctor again—the one who had prescribed tranquilizers in 2000. He made it clear that without those tranquilizers I could die from stress. He talked about putting me on antidepressants too. I refused them but reluctantly agreed to take the tranquilizers at night. In lieu of antidepressants, I would continue counseling. I knew I needed to get off the tranquilizers, and I carried shame that I depended on them, a taboo in my childhood 12-step home. (As long as I knew him, my father was a recovered alcoholic. He was 63 years sober when he died in 2015.) I kept this part of my life secret from my parents and siblings. They would have certainly disapproved. I had to face my fears of disappointing my family.

I still wanted to prove that I could be successful and smart. And I worried constantly about what my husband, father, father-in-law, and my so-called business partners thought. The emotional scars from my past made me fear men. Over and over, I had lectured my daughters about not letting someone control or abuse them in any way. I wanted to keep my girls as safe as could be. I wanted them to stand up for themselves and live their lives the way they wanted to. I had reminded my son how important it was to treat women with respect, yet, sadly, I cannot remember telling him not to be a victim of someone else's control, manipulation, or abuse. I encouraged him to follow his dreams but grew anxious when he talked about his future. He wanted to leave home someday and travel the world. I couldn't bear the thought. All these things weighed heavily on my mind. At least with tranquilizers I could sleep at night when my anxiety was the worst.

On my way home from the doctor's office, a filled prescription of tranquilizers on the passenger seat, I heard, "You do not need to prove yourself to anyone. Do what you want. Live authentically." *It is time to get rid of the business.* It was true! I didn't need to prove myself to anyone anymore.

As soon as I got home, I ran down to my studio and called a non-profit organization, which, for the life of me, I cannot remember the name of, and arranged to donate all the cards to their fundraising efforts. I packed them into my car and drove to Denver to deliver them. After I had put the last box of cards in their office, I walked out the door, feeling lighter and more self-assured. I knew, without a doubt, what I was supposed to do—focus on writing Chipeta's story and working on my own life.

Never had a project affected me in such a way. Chipeta and the Ancestors were ever-present. They constantly pulled me into the past, so I found it harder and harder to live in the present. The dreams and predawn visitations continued. These dreams were so vivid I smelled the Ancestors' buckskin and tobacco. What *else* did they want from me? Hadn't I done enough?

I kept my experiences from Mark. Instead, wrote about them in my journal where they were kept hidden. We limited our topics of conversation to kids, family, the mechanics of my writing, and other safer subjects. He would be frustrated with me, and yet he seemed to roll with the punches as my businesses succeeded or failed. He was often more supportive of me than I gave him credit for. I just would not accept that he did not understand the transcendent events taking place in my life.

***

I knew the Ute migrated to the cooler climate of the mountains during the warm weather. I could relate to the experiences Chipeta might have had as a little girl as they camped in the mountain meadows. Our family made many summer trips to the mountains near Nathrop, Colorado. It was not hard to imagine young Chipeta sitting around a campfire under the stars at night in the cool mountain air. I envisioned her listening raptly to the stories told by elders. This was how Chipeta and other children in the tribe learned their histories. My own parents shared stories too, as we sat around a campfire under the starry night sky.

It was difficult to read how Ute territories diminished dramatically due to treaties that were not honored and the relentless influx of non-Indigenous. How awful that the government forced the Ute from lands that the Creator had put them on. I grieved for Chipeta, Ouray, and the Ute losing a traditional way of life, and for the children later forced into boarding schools. I would be reading about treaties and broken promises, and I would experience an intense disappointment for Chipeta and Ouray and the Ute people. I'd also viscerally experienced Chipeta's love for Ouray's baby boy and the love and respect she had for her husband Ouray.

Each morning before I wrote, I prayed for Chipeta, Ouray, Pahlone, the Ancestors, my new Ute friends, for CJ and her family, Roland and his family as well, and for all Indigenous nations. I asked Chipeta to guide me through the maze of historic data—the majority recorded by non-Indigenous—and the stories told by Roland and other members of the Ute tribes I had the privilege to meet.

With her help, my manuscript slowly but surely began taking shape. I wrote pages and pages of her story. Every so often my inner critic would rear its ugly head to remind me I did not have enough education to do the job. Was I equipped to put her history into words? It had taken me forever to get my library card at the age twenty-one, and to begin reading in earnest. (I had undiagnosed dyslexia, which made reading difficult.) Would Chipeta's book be scholarly enough?

In *Hiking through Colorado History*, I wrote about the plight of the Ute, about the tribes losing their lands. I was honest but kept the descriptions short and sterile. Now I was writing a history that I could no longer gloss over. I knew that I would need to share this with everyone. I often asked myself what I was doing writing such a story. I had gone out a limb and bought a car, driven to meet

Chipeta's descendants and heard their side of her life's story. I had listened carefully and written down all the information I could. I spent hours reading my notes, visiting historical archives, poring over microfilm, and more. Was that enough background to qualify me to write this book? I was not always sure. Still, I trusted Chipeta and the Ancestors and, more important, refused to dishonor my sacred agreement with them. Even though I was often uncomfortable, I continued to write.

I traveled for school visits, I constantly visited historical libraries and museums, antique shops, or used bookstores. I gathered census data, treaty documents, and anything else I could find that at all related to Chipeta and the Ute. I kept a binder (later, seven binders) and divided it up into sections and combined the sections with my photocopies of images and stories. Slowly the shelves in my studio filled with research materials.

June 24, 2002

As I work, I do know that my "prolific and brilliant writer," Vickie Leigh will show up! [An affirmation I used to boost my confidence] *It is natural for me to write this book. I AM a part of Chipeta's family. She opened the door of her home for me to come to this place in history and time, and to meet her great, great grandson and descendants. I have been open, and I will stay open. I will write this book from the heart.... I am safe, and I will be taken care of. God and Chipeta, I feel such gratitude for all the things I have. I am thrilled that I can use my creative gifts to understand the past...*

One morning that month, while I was writing about Chipeta, I heard something that sent panic shooting through me. *"You will go on a courage journey."* The words were simple yet terrifying. It was Chipeta asking me to do the impossible, travel alone to Montrose to finish my book. I knew I was *not* to take my mother or sister when I drove to the Ute Indian Museum in late October. *No! Not that!* I thought. *I cannot do it.*

I had nearly finished the first draft of the manuscript. Why did she mention a courage journey at this stage? *What if it snows on the mountain passes? What if my car breaks down? What if something happens to me?* Despite my worst case scenario thinking, I knew that I had to listen to Chipeta. It was time to rely on my ability to take care of myself and trust that I would survive such a trip. Plus, I trusted Chipeta. I called CJ and let her know I would be in Montrose in October. I did not know the exact dates yet.

Did Chipeta know I needed time to prepare myself for the courage journey, that I needed to process her request and plan? Yet, her request was clear, and I knew I could not ignore it. It was obvious I needed to end my manuscript where I started it, on the Ouray Memorial Park grounds, site of the Ute Indian Museum and Chipeta and Ouray old homestead at the Los Piños II Agency.

Chapter Thirteen
A Funeral and a Feast

By mid-summer 2002, my research materials were well organized and brimming with information about Chipeta's life. Book chapters about her early and middle years had taken shape, and it was time to move into her later years, including her life on the reservation and her death on August 17, 1924. In her last years, she was blind, and all but forgotten by the United States government. It had promised to build her a home like the one she and Ouray had built at the Los Piños II Agency (in present day Montrose), but it never materialized. However, the United States government did build a fine white house for the officers, barracks for the soldiers, and stables for their horses on the Uintah-Ouray reservation. The government hadn't honored their promise to Chipeta. Instead, they gave her a small wood structure that eventually became a storage shed. She had preferred the traditional teepee to that of the small unfinished building.

CJ told me the Ute Indian Museum and Friends of the Ute were hosting Chipeta Day on August 17, to mark the 78th anniversary of Chipeta's death. She invited me to attend and speak about my book project. "Of course, I'll come," I said without hesitation. It would have been a shame not to, as I would get to mingle with living descendants of Chipeta's extended family. "Bring your family," CJ said.

"Sure," I replied. *But will they come?* I asked myself.

I decided I would donate $500 of my book advance to the Friends of the Ute, to further their educational programming. My advance had not been all that large, but I felt giving this amount was the least I could do for the museum. I was concerned about how Mark might react to this, though. His support for my book project had grown, he had asked questions about my progress, and had often encouraged me while I wrote. I appreciated this. It was great, but.... I held my breath when I asked him about making this donation. He said it was a good idea. But that was not all. He also said he would take a long weekend and he and the kids would go to Montrose with me. Elated, I wasted no time making reservations for us at the Holiday Inn Express in Montrose where I had stayed with Mom and Valorie. I would finally have the chance to share my experiences with Mark and the kids.

Three weeks before our trip, I had another dreamtime visit with Chipeta. There were times when my dreams troubled me. I was constantly fixated on what I was supposed to write. When I begin writing the book in earnest, I had received a message from Chipeta, reminding me when I was in Montrose and the Uncompahgre Valley I was walking in the footsteps of the Ancestors. Thinking of these things I got up to journal, to put my concerns into words, and then Chipeta's familiar presence filled the room. She was next to me.

August 3, 2002

Moccasin-clad feet walked the paths that you speak of. We walked from Ouray to the Uncompahgre Valley to spend our summers gathering and hunting. Life as we knew it was good. When the Spanish came in the 1500's, Utes befriended them, and we learned from them. Then came others from the east. They did not stop.

They did not want to share the land. We carried our possessions and heartaches with us. We could not speak our minds to your government. We had no voice. Now you offer us the opportunity to bring these thoughts and feelings to the attention of government officials and to help us heal from our painful past. The meadow [Meeker Incident] was the beginning of our end. We farmed and lived like whites, yet whites became jealous of our accomplishments. Our people struggled with this way of life. They felt betrayed. We felt uncertainty and desperation to stay in our beloved valley. Two worlds, both hostile places.

What offering shall I make Grandmother?

Make a medicine bundle and fill it with sage, coffee, sweet grass, cornmeal, and whatever your heart tells you. Leave it at my grave early on the 17th. I will accept this gift and be your guide. Sleep well. Be peaceful. I love you, Granddaughter. You are safe and well! Ouray and I watch over you.

The next morning, I did as Chipeta instructed. I carefully cut a square of softened deer skin that I had purchased at a shop somewhere during my research trips. I lovingly placed her requested items on it and tied it shut. I would lay this at Chipeta's tomb.

The day before the trip I journaled: *I am filled with wonder and joy about my new discoveries and how they all fit together.*

My family and I left for Montrose on a Friday morning. We loaded our suitcases into the trunk of Mark's car and climbed into our seats. Mark turned the key in the ignition, but the engine would not turn over. He grimaced. "We'll just have to take my car," I said breezily. Mark and I still had our differences about my car, and he had refused to drive it or even ride in it. Well, this morning, he did not have a choice. Tightlipped, he switched the luggage from his car to mine, and then we were off.

We stopped to eat lunch in Grand Junction and reached Montrose that afternoon. After we had checked into our hotel, we drove over to the Ouray Memorial Park grounds, where we looked at teepees, Chipeta's tomb, and the grave of Chipeta's brother, John McCook, next to it. I showed my family where Chipeta and Ouray's adobe home once stood, and then we toured the Ute Indian Museum. Mark and the kids talked about the exhibits, and Jessica, our oldest, an anthropology student at the University of Colorado at the time, shared her knowledge about artifacts. While my family paid close attention, I talked about my encounters during my first visit to the museum. Here and there, I would say something about my spiritual experiences but chose to keep what I said light and logical. I secretly hoped they would have the same powerful experiences I had had.

We ate dinner out and then went back to the hotel, where we enjoyed family time in the pool. Mark and the kids were proud of me. I knew this because they told me. I felt happy and confident.

The next morning, we ate a quick breakfast, then headed over to the Ute Indian Museum, where Ute vendors had already set up on the lawn just outside the Chipeta Room. They displayed beautifully handcrafted jewelry, beadwork, and Ute Mountain Ute pottery decorated with traditional Ute designs. Chairs and a podium had been set up in front of Chipeta's tomb.

CJ introduced me to Ute guests, and most were kind to me but reserved. Others kept their distance. There was one guest I approached by myself, and before I could tell her my name, a younger woman pushed the older woman away from me. She scowled at me. I knew she was wary of this white woman and her intentions. It would be untruthful to say everyone embraced me.

When it was time, I joined the dignitaries from the Ute Mountain Ute tribe, Southern Ute, and the Northern Ute tribes. I had worn a black dress, which I thought was appropriate for a funeral reenactment and a way to show Chipeta respect. Other participants had dressed the same way. The sun beat down on us and me in my black dress. Beads of sweat formed on my forehead and neck and dripped down my back. No one complained about the heat, so I, too, kept my complaints to myself.

When select individuals from the different tribes gathered in front of Chipeta's tomb, CJ and Roland directed the rest of us to line up along a pathway to the right. No one spoke, as it was a time of introspection, prayer, and remembering Chipeta's return to Montrose following her death in Bitter Creek, Utah. Her family had buried her remains in a secret resting place, but someone had found them and suggested to her brother, John McCook, that he move her remains, so coyotes or rainstorms would not damage them.

When Montrose citizens heard about this discovery, they asked her brother to bring Chipeta's body home to Montrose. John had her remains exhumed and taken to Dragon, Utah. There Chipeta's body was laid in a simple wooden casket. On March 15, 1925, Chipeta's casket was loaded onto a train and transported to Montrose. Nearly 5,000 Ute and citizens from the town and surrounding areas waited for her arrival. Once Chipeta's casket arrived it was loaded onto a horse drawn wagon which took the body to the mortuary in town. A mile-long funeral procession followed the wagon. Later Chipeta's body was transported from the mortuary to the old homestead. She would be laid to rest where she, Ouray, and their adopted children had lived prior to their forced removal to Utah following Ouray's death. Chipeta's body was placed in the concrete tomb while the townspeople and Ute people watched.

On August 17, 2002, Chipeta's descendants joined the funeral procession. They all lined up in front of her tomb, and I joined them. I felt fortunate I was part of this small historic event. The fact that I was adding to my own history was not lost on me.

Ute drummers started the ceremony of remembrance. Their drumming and prayerful songs lifted into the morning air and blended with the buzzing of cicadas in nearby trees. I thought about Chipeta and her brother and how they must have been pleased to hear such earnest songs.

The procession walked slowly and wordlessly to Chipeta's tomb and sat down in the chairs provided for us. Someone said a prayer in Ute, and then Chipeta's descendants shared stories about her kindness and her love for others. They also spoke of her generosity. For example, in 1918, while living on the reservation in Bitter Creek, she had donated almost all of her life's savings, $300, to the Red Cross to help train nurses and help fight the Spanish flu epidemic. She fed the hungry and took loving care of children and adults alike, regardless of their race.

I was nervous when it was my turn to speak. I do not remember exactly what I said, other than I had been called to write the book, that I had a dream, and that I was grateful for its resulting journey. I said I wanted Chipeta's history told from the point of view of the People and not that of a non-Indigenous person. Then I presented my donation check, and the ceremony ended. Some members of the Ute tribes approached me asking me about my book. Others stayed away. I understood that it would take time to earn their respect.

Friends of the Ute invited all of us to feast on roast buffalo and side dishes. That was when I had my first taste of delicious, tender buffalo meat. In my mind's eye, I saw Ute hunting parties searching for buffalo on the eastern plains of Colorado. I imagined the hunters roasting their buffalo over a fire and feasting on it. It was thrilling to have my first taste of buffalo meat!

Chipeta Day activities filled the day. My favorite activity was watching Ute dancers perform on the lawn, surrounded by spectators from the tribes, the Montrose community, and from neighboring areas. Male and female dancers, young and old, wore handmade regalia that was so beautiful it took my breath away. The dancers' movements clearly expressed their love for their culture and traditions and expressed their connection to Chipeta and all their Ancestors. After two or three dances, they invited the spectators to participate in a friendship dance. Under a canopy of cottonwood trees silhouetted by bright blue skies, my family and I joined hands with the dancers and other audience members and stepped sideways to the beat of the drums, dancing in a circle of friendship.

Wiesbaden Hot Springs and Spa in Ouray, Colorado. The Ute soaked in the hot springs inside the caves to heal their bodies and strengthen them. Horses, too, were brought in to be healed and blessed. 2003.

The next morning, Sunday, my family, and I drove to Ouray. I wanted us all to soak in the vapor caves at Wiesbaden Hot Springs and Spa. Again, I was the tour guide and storyteller. I used Roland and CJ's words to tell my family about the history and important sites along the way. On Highway 50, I had Mark pull the car to the side of a road so I could point out where Fort Crawford once stood, a reminder of the once ever-present United States cavalry in the new Los Piños II Indian Agency. Next, we traveled toward Ridgway, where the Ute often summered to avoid the heat and, I am sure, to hunt game and gather plants. I pointed out the meadows where Ute ponies had grazed. I felt a renewed emotional bond to every location.

Once at the Wiesbaden Hot Springs and Spa, I explained to my family the history and importance of the caves. When we entered the caves, we kept our voices low and gave ourselves time to experience the atmosphere and acclimate to the water. This time, I could not discern the face on the wall. And I heard no prayers or chanting. Yes, I was disappointed. I had told my children about what I had experienced there in April, but they did not bring it up. We were simply tourists visiting an interesting place.

After our soak, we relaxed around the outdoor pool encircled by the crimson cliffs of Ouray. With this, my longing for a deep and meaningful connection with Mark, my family, and my home grew stronger. I could have stayed there forever, but I wanted to get back to my writing. We would all have to go back to Denver and resume our busy lives, go back to life as usual. Well, not all of us would go back to life as usual. Too much had changed for me.

I reflected on the Chipeta Day celebration when we got home: *Montrose was interesting and yet did not feel the same as it did in April. Mark told Jessica he could really "feel" the drums deep inside his body. He seemed interested, yet cautious with his emotions. Logic was oozing from his pores, yet I sensed his desire to simply let go and enjoy.*

I had wished Mark would have had the same response to Montrose and Ouray as I had. He had not. Our differences in what we believed truly bothered me. I needed him to take the same journey I was taking. I still wanted him to validate what I was feeling and experiencing. He could not, though. But I know he tried.

Chapter Fourteen

The Train to Nowhere

Another new year, 2003, arrived. It would be the year I would complete *Searching for Chipeta*. Words and stories about Chipeta and the Ute poured onto the pages of my manuscript. I had written about the Meeker Incident as Roland had recounted it at the Ute Indian Museum in 2001. I still needed chapters about Chipeta and the Uncompahgre Ute traveling to Washington, D.C. for the Meeker hearings in 1880. I also needed a chapter about Ouray's death and about Chipeta and the Ute tribe being forcibly removed from Montrose and marched to a reservation in northeastern Utah in 1881. I decided to visit the Uintah-Ouray Reservation, but only with permission. Roland had agreed to meet me there on February 19, at Fort Duchesne. I would travel by train, so that I might have an understanding what train travel was like for Chipeta, Ouray, and the Ute delegation in January 1880, when they traveled to Washington, D.C. My mother readily agreed to go with me. She was eager to see Valorie and travel with us to see Roland.

On the morning we departed from Denver, Mark drove us to Union Station. I looked west at the snow-covered mountain tops. I had no idea what to expect. Apart from a short and smoky ride on the Durango-Silverton Railroad while vacationing with my family in southwest Colorado (a tourist destination), I had never ridden on a passenger train.

I kissed Mark goodbye, and Mom and I stepped onto the train platform at Union Station in Denver. I handed my suitcase to a porter and climbed into the California Zephyr. The train rumbled and shook underneath my feet when I climbed aboard. It jerked as it left Union Station, moving through the Denver metro area and into the nearby foothills of Boulder, Colorado. It moved west and soon we were behind the famous Boulder Flatirons and into the middle of the Rocky Mountains. This was another surreal moment for me. I could not believe the things I was doing to get at the center of Chipeta's life and times.

Mom and I were fortunate that this February's weather was unseasonably mild. The sun shone for us almost all the way to Utah. In January 1880, the Uncompahgre Ute traveling to D.C. were not so lucky. This delegation, which included Chipeta and Ouray, other tribal leaders, and government officials, road on horseback or on buckboards over the steep San Juan Mountain passes and towards Alamosa. Heavy snows and freezing temperatures made travel risky. Six-to-eight-foot snowdrifts made traversing the mountain passes and valleys treacherous. Finally, they reached Alamosa and boarded a train for Pueblo, Colorado.

The passenger car Mom and I rode in was massive. I tried to imagine petite Chipeta climbing up the metal stairs that led to a car like this. It must have been unnerving and unnatural for her to feel the rumbling underneath her feet. Our rail car was warm, and it had comfortable seats and headrests. There were bathrooms, a dining car, and an observation car made mostly of windows. Shortly after our trip started, Mom and I got an inexpensive upgrade on our tickets. The cost was minimal, which was great, because I had a limited travel budget. This allowed us to ride in a private car with a berth and take meals in the dining car. There had been no such thing for the Ute delegation headed east to Washington, D.C.

The scenery through the Rockies was spectacular—especially because we rode in sufficiently warm cars, which was vastly different from what Chipeta, Ouray, and the Ute delegation traveled in. Historical accounts of her experience helped me envision old train windows encrusted in thick ice, with only a small stove to heat the train car. We stopped two or three times because of snow slides or other trains being on the track. Nothing too perilous. At first, I enjoyed the train's rhythmic motion. The rocking motion of Chipeta's train made her sick. There was not a dining car for her or the delegation. Their only food and drink was what they had brought with them.

When their train stopped at the station in Pueblo, Colorado, hundreds of hostile spectators were waiting for them. As the delegation stepped down from the train, the mob screamed and threw rocks at them. The delegates were quickly ushered into a nearby depot, where they had an opportunity to eat and refresh themselves before heading eastward across the prairies.

With every subsequent change of scenery, I grew quieter and more introspective. Snow drifts rose high along the tracks and the mountainsides. I could not begin to imagine was it was like to ride a horse or wagon through the San Juan Mountains in January, like Chipeta and Ouray, and the delegation did, to reach the train in Alamosa. I had known how lush the mountains were in late spring, summer, and autumn, and now from the windows of our train, I would witness their winter beauty. My train carried me snuggly from my home north of Denver to Utah. Chipeta's train carried her uncomfortably from her beloved home in Colorado to the east coast and an ambiguous future. There must have been a sense of foreboding as they made their way eastward.

I put the Ute creation story in the first chapter of *Searching for Chipeta*. Sinawaf, the Creator, had given the Ute the lands I now rode through. Sinawaf made all the people out of sticks. They were of all colors. He put them in a pouch and asked his brother, Coyote, not to

***We Have Been Here for as Long as We Can Remember. The Ute Creation Story.* Artwork by Vickie Leigh Krudwig. 2005.**

touch the bag. Coyote did not listen. He let the people out of the bag, and they scattered in The Four Directions. Sinawaf noticed that some stick people had not run away. So, he made them brave and strong and placed them in the mountains, so they would always be close to their Creator. The Ute still say, "We've been here as long as we can remember."

In the summer, the Ute migrated throughout the Four Corners region and up into the high mountain valleys. There, Chipeta, like other young girls, would receive her digging stick. She learned early on how to identify and harvest hundreds of plants for food and medicine. These plants were abundant on the hills and in the valleys of the Rocky Mountains. They were the difference between life and death for the People during the long winter months or when they were hungry or sick.

Just as the sun was getting ready to set, our train crossed over the Colorado River and into Utah. The Ute had crossed this river when calvary soldiers marched them toward the Uintah-Ouray reservation, near present day Fort Duchesne, in east central Utah. Our train lurched, and I looked out the window at an unrecognizable landscape, a drastically altered one. It was like we were nowhere. I felt as though someone had punched me in the stomach. The farther west we traveled, the more withdrawn I grew. My mom's and my unease were palpable. With tears in my eyes, I turned to Mom and said, "How could we do such a thing?"

All the historical accounts I had read and heard about this land were all too real. The land before me was as stark as anything I had ever seen. Except for an occasional stand of rabbit brush or clump of dry grass, there were no grasses or bushes. There were no trees to shelter the people from the elements. I saw no sources of water. The Northern Ute (Tabeguache band) and the White River Ute were forced to relocate here.

The United States government had initially planned to move the Ute to a reservation near present-day Grand Junction. But unscrupulous officials told the government that if they determined the land was unfit for habitation, they would move the Ute elsewhere. The lands were excellent for farming, but the officials lied. They said the region did not have enough water nor farmland to support the tribes. Once again, government officials had misled the people. They had manipulated the move to Utah, so they could open the lands to non-indigenous settlers and farmers. Even today, I can barely stand to drive through the region without thinking of the Ute people and how the United States government cheated them out of such productive land. It makes me sad.

The Ute people walked into the interior of the reservation in late September 1881, a little more than a year after the hearings in Washington, D.C., and Ouray's death. There were little to no plants for the women to harvest, or game. *Without game and traditional plants how did the Ute men and women feed and care for their families?* I wondered. *How could these barren lands support so many?* I felt great shame for the way the United States government had wronged and cheated the Ute. I now understood what Roland meant. The more I learned about the reservations and the hardships the Ute faced, the heavier my burden of guilt and the greater my sadness for the actions taken against them.

Unable to comprehend the horrific conditions the Ute faced, Mom and I rode the rest of the way in silence. I was glad when the moon came out and darkness shrouded the barren landscape. Still, the silhouette of the nightscape reminded me of what the Ute tribes had lost. I tried to sleep, but the motion of the train and the reality of Chipeta's life made me queasy.

***The photographic mural seen in the Chipeta Room at the Ute Indian Museum during my first visit in 2002,* showed the Ute moving to the Uintah-Ouray Reservation in Utah in 1881.**

I wrote in my journal, but the entry needed only one page. I scribbled it in haste. I could not continue writing the words.

February 18, 2003

I look out of the train window at a rugged and barren landscape—save a few thousand clumps of sagebrush. I sit in a private room, on a train headed to Salt Lake City, Utah. As we ride through the mountains, I think of you, Chipeta, and Ouray, and the rest of your entourage as you boarded the train to Washington, D.C. I ride in quiet comfort and dine in a formal dining car. I cannot help thinking of your train ride, the first long trek on a long, long journey across the country. You are on your way to testify before congress about Old Man Meeker, as you all called him, and the incident that took place as the Utes were being forced to conform to their ways.

I set my pen down and closed my journal. There was too much to process, and words were not adequate. I simply had to be still and let the sights and sounds of the past months settle inside me, let them become part of my own history in this time and place. I would never again see the west as I had when I was young.

I was relieved when we arrived in Salt Lake City. It was 1:00 a.m. and Mom and I were glad to disembark, as it had been a long 17-hour ride to reach the Great Basin of Utah. I wondered how long it had taken the Ute delegation to get to Washington, D.C. Valorie and her husband, Garry, met us at the train station. They helped us load our suitcases into their car and then they drove us to their house. There we chatted briefly, then headed for our beds. I was exhausted and eager to sleep. When I placed my head on the pillow and closed my eyes, I was dizzy and could still feel the motion of the train.

I could not stop thinking about Chipeta, her then sickly husband Ouray, and the Ute delegates as they stepped off the train in Washington, D.C. How strange this must have been for them. Newspapers printed fantastical stories about them, and society people invited Chipeta, Ouray and the Ute delegates to gatherings. They called Chipeta "Queen of the Utes" because of the Meeker Incident and Eugene Fields' exaggerated poem. It turned out the government hearings they attended did nothing to save the balance of their homelands.

Early that morning, Mom, Valorie, and I headed south in Valorie's car to Fort Duchesne. I carefully studied the passing landscape, as I was not a tourist but a traveler through time. I was a little nervous as we approached the reservation. Just before we pulled into the lot near the tribal headquarters, Val, Mom, and I were startled to see three bald eagles standing by the roadside. I had never seen them up close like this. It felt surreal to me.

Ouray, chief of the Native American Utes, and his wife, Chipeta, pose for their last formal portrait together in Washington, D. C. in January 1880 at the Walker Art Studio. Ouray wears braids, a choker, fringed buckskin shirt, a breech cloth, leggings, and boots. Chipeta wears a fringed buckskin dress, a necklace with a cross, leggings, and moccasins. **Denver Public Library Special Collections (X-30600)**

We met Roland at the tribal headquarters of the Uintah -Ouray Reservation. Roland took us on a brief tour of the reservation and surrounding areas. He showed us the officer's quarters, barracks, and stables for the soldiers' horses. The white buildings reminded me of the very first dream I had about Chipeta.

Roland reminded us of how the Ute had to adapt to the harsh climate—one that did not provide the much-needed plants and animals the Ute had always depended upon when they lived in Colorado. The home the government promised to build Chipeta was never finished. At the end of our tour, Roland bid us farewell, and my mom, sister, and I all made our way back to Valorie's house. All the way up the highway we talked about the history of the Ute people, the settlement of the west and its destructive toll it had on the Ute. Still the Ute prevailed despite interference from non-Indigenous people.

Chapter Fifteen

Well Worth the Journey

It had been several months since my trip to the Uintah-Ouray Reservation. I continued to write about Chipeta, keeping all the things I learned from her relatives, tribal members, and my own visit to Utah, in mind. This was a crucial part of Chipeta's life, and that of the Ute people. I re-read my research documents, reviewed historical photos, talked to CJ and Roland often, and moved forward. I spent hours rewriting the chapters that would soon become Chipeta's story.

I submitted a first draft to Susan Hill-Newton, my editor at Fulcrum Publishing Company. I was anxious to hear from her. A few weeks later, Susan and I met for breakfast to discuss the manuscript. It sat on the table in front of me. I was a nervous wreck. I waited for her to speak. Susan said she liked my first four chapters the best because they gave readers a personal glimpse of Chipeta as a wife and mother. After that, Susan said the chapters became less personal and seemed to be detached from Chipeta herself. After our meeting I took the marked-up manuscript and drove home.

I considered the comments from Susan. I had become detached from the personal side of Chipeta's life. This is how I had usually dealt with difficult situations with relationships, with Mark, my parents, Mark's parents, and sometimes even with my kids. During these times I could hardly stay within my own physical and mental boundaries. I seemed to disassociate with myself and my life. I would feel strangely numb and out of my body.

Sometimes these episodes made their appearances while in counselling, and at night when I was alone with my thoughts. It was in those lonely moments that I evaluated my life, my decisions, and my fears of being alone. I also knew my days of controlling my children and trying to control Mark were coming to an end. I felt it to my core. Now, I was dealing with Chipeta's life and times and trying to put her experiences into words that readers would relate to.

I often wondered about Chipeta's situation and that of the Ute when the United States government broke treaties and seemed to control their destiny. It was for the Ute's benefit, the officials had said. It looked as if the United States government said they wanted to *discuss* things with the Ute when they had already *decided* the outcomes. Unlike the Ute, I had the opportunity to choose my future. The thought of it scared the hell out of me.

I continued to think and write about my experiences since my first dream. I talked to CJ and Roland about the first time we met and the blessing we received in the cave. We all wished we wished he could hear the voice again. I knew what they meant. The experience was both powerful and soothing. I relived my experience with the strange woman who sat next to me in the dressing room, comforting me. Her voice was clear, strong, low, and slow. (It is still with me.) I remembered thinking at the time that she was Indigenous, a younger version of Chipeta. Was this the same voice I had heard in the cave?

September 22, 2003

Granddaughter. Pay attention. There is wisdom in the memory of the woman. She gave you a gift. The caves are filled with good things of the Ancestors. They heal the person both spiritually and physically. Yet, few understand. In April of next year, you must go again. Let us guide you. Your journey has just begun. Sleep well. Know that you, Roland, CJ, and the Ute people are in good hands. We see and acknowledge your good deeds. They are only the beginning. The road is long, but the journey is well worth it.

Now I wondered what I would being doing in April. I loved the idea of going back to Montrose in 2004. But why? I was certain all would be revealed in due time. That is how things worked. Until then, I would focus on getting the story done.

I had reviewed my collected documents and laid them out in my office. I had sorted the chapters of the book and attached them to my bulletin board that hung just above my desk. I had removed all the items on the board and placed them in a basket. On 3x5 inch index cards, I had written questions Susan and I had about the Ute way of life and Chipeta. I had created a timeline, and then, more importantly, decided to write the book as historical fiction. I would use facts from Chipeta's life as well as my childhood experiences of living in Colorado and playing in meadows where the Utes and other tribes had camped. I would write about the mountains and starry night skies. I would imagine Chipeta's love for her son, Pahlone, and her horror at losing him so suddenly. I would narrate using Chipeta's perspective as a child, a wife, a mother, and a widow.

From then on, the words flowed and flowed. I wrote from early morning until late at night, and sometimes into the wee hours of the following morning. I would fall into bed, exhausted but eager to resume my writing. Mark was incredibly supportive of my efforts, and so were the kids. Everyone pitched in with cooking and cleaning and giving me feedback when I read chapters to them.

I reviewed my journals and handwritten notes. I remembered stories shared by Chipeta's descendants about how little girls learned from their older sisters, aunts, mothers, and grandmothers. I reflected on Chipeta's first attempt at beadwork, on her caring for her little doll and getting her first digging stick. I remembered that she learned about life through play and through the stories of the elders. While I wrote, I felt immense love for her. When I would approach the sad and difficult times in her life, I let the emotions come. I acknowledged all the events that were part of her story, and, in the process, I acknowledged my own life's story. The two roads were merging in a way I could not have dreamed possible.

Then it was late fall and time to finish the rewrite of the last few chapters before I sent the manuscript to the publisher for a another round of editing. The closer my deadline, the greater the struggle with my inner critic. My writing desk was in the basement, where there were no windows and only a small space heater for warmth. It did not keep the deep chill out of my body. One night I was in tears when came up out of the basement. I had been agonizing over each word and change in the manuscript, and my hands and feet were freezing and cramped from the long hours at the keyboard. I had hit a wall of exhaustion.

During dinner, I told Mark I did not think I would get the manuscript done in time for the deadline. He listened patiently and then asked me how many more chapters I still had to do. I told him and then commented that the process was slow. I said it was too cold for me in the basement. Mark stood up and walked into the living room, moved the couch, and completely rearranged the room. Next, he helped me clear off my desk and carry it up the stairs to the living room and place it where the couch had been. Then came my computer, printer, office chair, and all my materials. He set up a lamp on my desk, so I had better visibility. By now my vision had changed significantly, so the extra light helped.

Because of Mark's actions, I felt an even closer bond with him. They filled me with gratitude for his encouragement and support. It came at a time when I was doubting myself and really needing to hear from him that I could complete my book. This rejuvenated me, and I was ready to see the project to its end.

Chapter Sixteen

Courage Journey

I held the steering wheel in the ten and two o'clock position while I waited for my blue Dodge Neon to warm up. It was Saturday morning, October 29, 2003. I shivered, not from cold but from apprehension. I was facing one of my biggest challenges in the project. I was going to Montrose to do my final phase of research and finish the book. *alone.* The time had come for my courage journey. I was pulled in too many directions, though I wanted and really needed the inspiration that only Chipeta's homelands could provide. I also wanted peace and quiet in which to work. Other authors found it. They retreated into silence as they typed their way through their final drafts of their manuscripts. So why couldn't I?

Once the engine warmed up, I put my car into gear and headed down my parents' long gravel driveway. On Friday, I sat down with my father in the living room and waited for his feedback and approval of my manuscript as I had written it so far. Agitated, he held it up and then set it down in his lap. "Hell, I could write shit better than this," he said. He told me I was trying too hard to sound scholarly. I cringed, anxious and full of shame. He suggested I stay at the ranch, and he would help me write my book. That meant he would assume the writer's role. I told him I had to write it alone.

Dad did not know I had written a different version in a more personal voice, one that drew upon my own thoughts and experiences as a young woman, mother, and wife. I had written it from the heart and lips of people who remembered Chipeta's valor, beauty, and strength. It was mine alone, and I could not share it with him, not then. Still, I had felt the need to be scholarly, so I wrote a second version in a scholarly fashion. So, after this truthful assessment of my manuscript, I knew what I would do. I go back to my first version of my manuscript and let Chipeta's story unfold.

Saturday morning, I left my mother and father sitting at their kitchen table, worried about my strange behavior. I was driving by myself to Montrose, and they disapproved. My mom had pursed her lips and said nothing. She had looked at my father and then at me. My father had said, gentler now, "We think you are running away from your life."

"Yes, I am running away," I told them. My tears flowed and my voice was bold and full of pain. I told them I was running away from my old fearful way of living, from being a worrywart. I had always had a safety net under me, the first being my twin sister, Veronica, the second being my mom and dad, and the third, my husband and kids. I had had a tremendous fear of being alone. I knew it was time to leave that part of my life behind. I told my parent that I *had* to make this trip. Chipeta had appeared to me again and insisted that I come "home" to Montrose. And yet, it was not only about the book, but it was also about spiritual and mental growth. For months I prepared myself mentally for the trip.

Through the window, my parents watched me put my suitcases in my car. I went back inside to kiss them goodbye and to reassure them I would be okay. Their faces still showed their disapproval.

I walked out the back door and, without looking back, got into my car. I slowly drove down their driveway, the gravel crunching underneath the tires. Anxiety washed over me. *Breathe* I told myself, *just breathe.* I pulled over just before the open gate at the end of the driveway. I watched southbound cars pass. To my right, Highway 115 stretched out before me. *Maybe they are right*, I thought. My family insisted that I had gone to extremes for this project. To drive by myself was unheard of.

I thought of Chipeta and the trials she had faced. She and her people had had countless confrontations with hostile and greedy miners, endured fruitless negotiations with the United States government, and suffered because of broken treaties. Chipeta had watched her husband slowly die from kidney disease, she had faced the prospect of life without him. I took a deep breath and slowly exhaled. If she could face such difficulties and uncertainty, so could I. It was now or never. I shifted my car into drive. I turned onto the highway and headed south. My courage journey had officially begun.

I can always pull off and turn around, I reasoned with myself when anxiety took over. *Just a few more miles. You can do it!* This inner dialogue continued as I made my way through the winding valleys along the Arkansas River. I fondly remembered my mother sitting next to me when I went to Montrose the first time. Now, her voice guided me again. It somewhat comforted me, but I still had mountains to climb, including Monarch Pass. I drove up and over the pass toward my destination.

One by one, I conquered the winding rock canyons and steep mountain passes. With each switchback I relived how fear had dictated my direction in the past. Dreams had not been realized because I was afraid to take chances, especially chances like this. I prayed to God to watch over me, and I asked Chipeta and the Ancestors to stay close.

Then I smelled pipe tobacco, and the hair on my arms and head stood up. I felt the presence of a man sitting in the passenger seat. Though I could not see him, I knew he was larger than life, and I knew he was my traveling companion. I was safe and protected. My prayers had been heard.

The Blanket. Artwork by Vickie Leigh Krudwig. 2005.

I watched quaking aspen leaves shimmer in the morning sun. I turned on my CD player and listened to Indigenous flute music. I rolled down the windows and breathed in the cool, crisp, pine-scented air. This was a spiritual experience. I had crossed the Continental Divide and was halfway to my destination. I had faced my fear of driving alone—if I considered having an invisible passenger as being alone. Somehow, and I do not know where it happened, wonder had replaced fear. I was safe, and the Heavenly Creator had taken care of me. I passed a cluster of small boulders on a hill just outside of Montrose, and, just like that, my traveling companion jumped out of the car.

Tears of joy ran down my face as I drove into the Uncompahgre Valley. Cottonwoods and willows blazed in splendor as the rich red and gold colors of fall wrapped themselves around the landscape. I had made it. I had really done it. I had finally come home alone!

Reclaiming my Life

My courage journey was almost at an end. I spent Friday afternoon and Saturday doing research and adding important dates and details to my manuscript so I could complete it. CJ and I visited from time to time, but my focus was on the book. I needed to wrap up the manuscript and get it to my editor. After a busy and fruitful day at the museum on Saturday, I went back to the hotel where I was staying. I grabbed dinner along the way and ate it in my hotel room. I took time to relax, and let the weekend sink in. Who could have imagined I'd be this brave to cross the mountains by myself and stay in a hotel alone? It felt like I was in someone else's body.

I felt a deep sense of satisfaction that I had followed my own heart. It had guided me during the past few years while I traveled, did interviews, and researched historical archives. I was to head home Sunday morning. I would stop and stay at my mother and father's house, then head back to Denver on Monday morning. I was just settling in for the night when the phone on the nightstand rang. It was CJ.

"Sister," said CJ, "Come to the house "Mooshie" (CJ's husband) is going to give you a blessing for your trip home." CJ gave me the address and directions to their new home that she and her husband were buying. Earlier that day, I met him for the first time. CJ invited me to see their new home they had just signed papers for, but I hadn't paid attention to the route we had taken. I was filled with joy for them. I hated driving at night, and again, I grew anxious about driving in an unknown area. Still, I knew I needed to be there. I wanted to receive the blessing so my courage journey could be sacred. I quickly made way over to their house.

When I arrived, CJ and Mooshie had set up a small area in the living room for our blessing. Mooshie was in the kitchen sorting through a small toolbox of sorts. It held certain sacred objects, including sweet grass and sage, and what I think was a large abalone shell. He placed some of the plants into the shell and brought it into the living room. We sat down on the floor. CJ. sat to my left, as was customary for family members, as I would learn later. The Medicine Man or Holy Person would sit on the right. Tucked between them, I felt an intense sense of love and connection to this family and to Chipeta, Ouray, John McCook, Roland, and to the Ute people. I smiled as I looked around the room. CJ's young daughter, Nizhoni, of six years or so, slept soundly next to us. She seemed unaware of the commotion next to her. The middle son, Dakota, nine years old, sat at the dining room table doing homework. He seemed concentrated in his efforts and paid little attention to the blessing ceremony about to begin.

"Heavenly Creator," CJ's husband began. His prayer was heartfelt and filled with gratitude for the new home they had, their first. He wept as he acknowledged such a gift, as well as for their family. Then Mooshie blessed me and my project, and the journey home. I was so moved as he made the prayer in the Navajo way and language. The air was filled with the sacred energies of the past, present, and future. I wept hard. It seemed like I was crying all throughout the project. I felt a deep sense of loss, too, after the blessing and CJ knew it.

She said it was going to be hard for me to leave. I was at the end of the book project and thought I wouldn't be back for a while. I was filled with sorrow for having to say goodbye and leave Montrose. I *was* home and I didn't want to go back to Denver. I wanted to stay where I was, where the museum and Chipeta were. I was afraid to go back home. What if I returned to my old way of living life? I could barely stand the thought. I didn't want the project to end.

The sun was barely up when I left Montrose for Denver. I wanted to be on the roads with less traffic. I put my things in the trunk of my car and closed it. When I reached the handle of my car door, I looked around me at the sleepy town of Montrose. I was really going to miss it, CJ and the Ute Indian Museum. I took a deep breath and climbed into my car. It was time to go back home and finish Chipeta's story. It was due in early December. The book would be released in early 2004.

I felt apprehensive as I headed east on Highway 50. I marveled at the beauty surrounding me that morning. Sunlight was glinting off the changing trees and rivers, making everything magical. I drove west and across the bridge on the Blue Mesa Reservoir, something that terrified me.

Still, I crossed over the structure. I stopped in Gunnison at a fast food restaurant for a bathroom break and breakfast, and a hot cup of coffee. Afterwards, I got back in my car and got back on the highway and headed east. I felt the familiar sense of anxiety as I continued my journey. In an hour or so I'd be facing Monarch Pass again.

I retraced the route I took to get to Montrose. At one point in the trip, I came to an area near the present-day town of Saguache. This was one of the regions set aside for the tribes following one of the early treaties with the United States government. The Los Piños Agency was established in the region and would be the new home of the Tabeguache Ute, but not for long. Miners trespassed onto the lands and continued to put pressures on the United States Government to open the area for mining. The Ute signed another treaty, the Brunot Treaty in 1879, and were moved to the Montrose area.

The morning was peaceful and quiet. The only sounds I heard were the gentle sounds of the bells worn by the sheep. 2003.

When I reached the turnoff or the town of Saguache, I pulled my car over to the side the road and got out. The sun was still low and illuminated some hills in the distance. The sheep I had seen the first time I traveled to Montrose, in 2002, still grazed in the meadow along the highway. In the stillness I took a deep and cleansing breath and listened intently. The only sounds I heard were the soft muted sounds of the bells tied around the necks of the sheep while they grazed.

I remembered how Ouray and Chipeta raised sheep at their farmstead in Montrose and farmed the land, at the encouragement of the United States government. Shortly after Ouray died, Chipeta was forced to leave her home. When the calvary forcibly marched the Ute to the Uintah-Ouray Reservation in Utah, Chipeta had taken the sheep with her. She settled near Bitter Creek, Utah, perhaps trying to be as close to Colorado as possible.

I don't know how long I remained at the fence watching the sheep and the changing light. I would never have gotten out of my car on any trip when I traveled alone for fear something might happen. And yet, here I was. Fearless and at peace at the scene before me. All felt right in the world. My soul was rested and grateful.

Back in my car, I put a Carlos Nakai CD into my car's player. His music filled my car. I cherished the sounds of the flute music, sheep bells, and the smell of sage and grass. My heart swelled and burst open with joy and acceptance of what was to come. I did tremolo at the top of my lungs. I didn't care if anyone heard me. I was reclaiming my power and my life! As I drove east on Highway 50, I heard a voice say loud and clear, *Now do you understand? The fear was never yours.*

Chapter Seventeen
Permission to Write

A month after my courage journey, I had yet another dream. In it I was walking shoulder to shoulder with men, women, and children from many tribes. They wore buckskin clothes that were so old there were no beads or quillwork on them. *Who are they?* I wondered. *Where are they going?* I did not know the answers, and they did not tell me. I just walked with them toward an unknown destination. The air was heavy. And then, without warning, these people crowded close to me, their mannerisms urgent, speaking in several different languages, they spoke louder and louder. Their numbers grew larger. I did not need to understand their words to know what they wanted. They pressed in tighter. They cried out. It was chaotic and stifling. Desperate, I raised my arms and spoke. “Listen,” I said, “I can only write one story at a time,” and then they vanished like smoke.

In the morning, I woke up feeling certain that Chipeta’s story was not the only story I would write. This thought sent a ripple of apprehension through me, yet I had to let it go. I needed to finish reviewing Susan’s editorial suggestions and make the necessary changes. I would have to wait and see what the future would hold.

My body felt poisoned from all the turmoil in my home, and I tried to keep my anger and sadness in check while I grieved my health. My days seemed hectic, and our family was in an upheaval. Rebecca and I argued about school, boyfriends, and I am not sure what else. Jessica was depressed and missed her boyfriend who had gone back to California to see his family. Still, she worked hard on the laundry and other household tasks while I worked. Benjamin was busy with after school activities. Mark was working long hours and helped wherever he could. It seemed I was in the doctor's office constantly.

A thyroid disease was causing havoc in my body, and I was experiencing chest pain and stomach issues. I had also developed pain in my lower jaw and underneath my tongue and in my salivary glands. Additionally, my businesses had failed, and so had my budgeting, leaving my family short of money every month. My anxiety attacks had become ferocious, and fear of illness and death formidable. I longed for my youth back and struggled to keep my focus on the good things in life. I had to remember I was not passive in this journey, as I had made my own path with the decisions I had made. I wanted to leave it all behind me and go back to Montrose.

I continued to have jaw and tongue pain, along with constant sore throats. When I could not stand the pain anymore, I met with an ear, nose, and throat specialist, who informed me I had stones inside my salivary ducts and under my tongue. He said I would need surgery. While I grappled with this news, I assumed the stones were related to my lifelong lack of self-expression. How many times had I kept my thoughts to myself when I genuinely wanted to speak? It seemed logical that my thoughts and unspoken words had turned to stone. I had a procedure to remove some stones, and even though my tongue and jaw were still sore, I felt better. But the "thoughts-turning-to-stone" image stayed with me.

Moreover, I lost the medicine pouch I had purchased from the Ute Indian Museum and was devastated. This felt like an omen.

I begin to read books on healing, chakras, about the energy system in the body. I read books by Caroline Myss, mystic and theologian, Sonjia Choquette, psychic and public speaker, Andrew Weil, M.D., and by other renowned experts in the fields of mysticism and physical and spiritual well-being. The more I read, the more I understood the changes taking place in my life. Somewhere deep inside me was a strong and vibrant woman who wanted to make herself visible to the world.

While pondering these things one morning, I wrote in my journal: *I fear being strong. Will it cause me more pain to be assertive? Where am I going? Where will the journey take me?* These questions and others kept me up nights. I would feel trepidation, then excitement. I knew I did not have to have all the answers, that I could seek help from those I trusted and from the heavenly realms. I asked Chipeta to help me find my medicine pouch and was so grateful when the pouch showed up a few days later. I was beyond happy to have this sacred object back and next to me while I wrapped up writing the book.

I showed up every day to write. Some days the words flowed effortlessly, and some days the words came slowly; perhaps they were waiting for me to process what I was saying on Chipeta's behalf. When I doubted myself, like writers do, I called upon my strong self to stay the course. Eventually, I completed the rough draft of *Searching for Chipeta* and handed it in to my editor, Susan. Now I would have to wait for her comments. I had hoped it was already good enough for publication. But when I got back the edited manuscript, I was embarrassed. Susan had not suggested any major changes, but I had wanted to give a perfect manuscript. I called her, and she and I discussed the changes. She assured me she intended her suggestions to help the book read better.

November 18, 2003

The wind has come up, and I am relishing the absolute quiet of the nighttime, except for a few chimes that are making enchanting, soothing sounds outside our window. Tonight, I spoke to Susan Hill, my editor, tonight regarding my rewritten manuscript. I was upset at her notes about my manuscript, yet I knew she was right. I was still struggling with the deep and intimate side of Chipeta's history, and my own.

As I talked to Susan, the word "permission" came into my mind, and I almost started sobbing. I knew at that moment I was struggling with the feeling I did not have permission to write the words to convey the life and times of Chipeta and the Ute. My culture was so different from that of Chipeta's and the Ute. I was witnessing her life through archives and the stories shared with me.

My dreams had been full of messages about the People, but I struggled with the fear of accepting these dreams at face value. They were so intense and so real I could not ignore them. My soul knew these visions and messages were possible, only Catholicism had made it clear to me that only saints, priests, and other holy people had these types of dreams and visions. Who was I to have such things?

Echoes in the Moonlight. Artwork by Vickie Leigh Krudwig. 2005.

In 2021, I took an online course, *The Power of Holy Language,* by Caroline Myss. Over the years I had participated in her online, audio, and in-person workshops. In *The Power of Holy Language*, she pointed out that too many of us live in our Earth bodies rather than in our soul bodies. Our Earth body limits us to material things and logic, while our soul body leaves at night, if it wants to, visits or communicates with the spiritual realm. Our soul is mystical, it represents our holy self. Me? With a holy soul? After all my life's ups and downs? As I have said, I had always had a deep spiritual connection to the world, even as a child. But adults and religious leaders around me stifled that. After I would share my dreams with them, they would say my dreams were just in my imagination or caused by something else. Their answers shielded me from naysayers and persons who only believed in the logic of an organized world. But I had always known the soul was mystical and full of grace.

Because of others' reactions, I had been afraid of the dreams and visions. But the dreams made my connection to Chipeta's life real, and they made me realize how much I had lost over the years. Writing her story brought forth raw emotions I hardly knew what to do with. When I downplayed the intimate aspects of Chipeta's story, I was trying to protect myself from her pain and mine.

Unable to sleep one evening, I got up and went into the family room. I opened my beaded medicine pouch and examined its contents: tiny twigs and bits of leaves from the Delta Council tree, a crystal, a bit of sage and sweet grass, and a small black pebble I had picked up along the Uncompahgre River. Oh, what sacred things! I lovingly put all but the black stone back in the pouch. I held the pouch up to my nose and inhaled. I could still smell piñon and sage smoke from the Ute Indian Museum, and it comforted me. I let my soul take over.

November 29, 2003

Is it me who shut down on you, Chipeta? I have felt such an emptiness and grief, and I miss your presence terribly. I long for the moments in Montrose and in Ouray when your presence was bigger than life. I am writing your life, Grandmother, to honor you, and to tell the truth. I write with sadness as I pore over my choice of words to describe sadness, heartache, betrayal, and grief.

I weep when I see you caring tenderly for Pahlone after Black Mare's death. I see you feeding him and washing his tiny body. I have written thousands of words, yet few can really capture you and your history. I can only surmise.

I ask for your forgiveness if I have offended you in any way—I seek only the truth and answers from your past. I am willing to keep my heart and mind open. I give you my talents and abilities, that you and your Ancestors might have a voice. Grandmother, I love you so very much. I am humbled and grateful for your presence in my life. I hold your tiny black pebble, as a gesture to be open to your wisdom.

At this point, I felt compelled to slip the pebble into my mouth. Why? I am not sure. But the following words in my journal made it clear: *The rock tastes like the earth and smells like the earth. I put it in my medicine pouch with sage, juniper, and sweet grass....*

I was connected to something bigger and sacred. I was of the Earth and sky and water. I was aware of expanding into a singular consciousness with the Universe.

After I had poured my soul into the pages of the journal, a presence filled the room, and I no longer felt alone. A familiar energy surrounded me—Chipeta. Her words came quietly but firmly.

November 29, 2003 (continued)

The permission comes from you. You hold back, fearful and lacking in self-confidence. When you met me in my dream (your dream) you were given the power to know certain things. You have experienced many extraordinary events, and you have become close to CJ, Mooshie, Roland, and CJ's children Amerson, Dakotah, and Nezhoni. You do know... you must let your inner voice guide you on this journey. Do not write for your father or mother but for all the pain and sadness you have been privileged to experience. Write from your own experiences—caring for your children, loving them so intensely that you cannot fathom a life without them. Write with your mind closed and your heart wide open. Let the channels be open... that you write unfettered, fearless, and full of compassion.

Granddaughter, I did not leave you. It was time for you to sort your thoughts. You needed to acknowledge your own fears, your own grief, your own betrayals, your own heartache, anger, resentment, and finally understanding. Without your own acknowledgements, you were not equipped to write about mine. Remember to keep the Sacred Circle in mind as you write spiritually and on earthly time, as the seasons marked the life and times of the Ute.

When we were to winter in the San Juans, we then had to adjust to winters in Saguache [site of the First Los Piños Agency]. *Instead of beading and playing games in the firelight, Ouray and I traveled thousands of miles away from home, confronted by another reality. Go ahead, acknowledge it, embrace it. Give your heart room to grow. It is like your trip to Montrose, you have no map, but you do know the way. I am with you. Listen, listen, and listen, your heart must be heard above all else. Let go of all other matters. Sleep and dream. You will rise to meet us, you will write, and you will be part of our story. You were there, and you have been given a connection. Allow the wisdom to flow freely through you. Wear your moccasins and your medicine pouch. There is power in your visions and dreams. Pay attention and act accordingly.*

I heard Roland's words again. "This will be a blessing and a burden." The hair on my arms and neck stood up, and I shivered. I knew I could not turn away from these dreams any longer. I set my pen down and closed my journal. I climbed into bed and lay awake in the dark, thinking about the words I had written. I knew then what I needed to do. I would get up early and begin revising Chipeta's story, and I would let my heart be the guide. I would speak the truth of what I learned about Chipeta and her people. Still, I had one more journal entry to make.

I had been revising the chapter about the Meeker Incident and had already revised a section about the Sand Creek Massacre when it dawned on me that it was the anniversary of that horrifying massacre. I remembered hearing from Roland how the Sand Creek Massacre stayed in the minds of the Ute people. (I would later meet and work with direct descendants of Cheyenne and Arapaho people who had narrowly survived the horrific Sand Creek Massacre,1864, and the Battle of Washita, 1868.)

November 29, 2003 (continued)

It is the 139th anniversary of the Sand Creek Massacre that I have been writing about, yet I had not made the connection until today. It has been a grueling week, and I have struggled to finish my book. I have agonized over every word, every sentence, every paragraph.... My body and mind are exhausted, and I am anxious to see this book through.

I could not imagine what the Ute were thinking then. It was a dark time for all Indigenous people living in and around Colorado. It was the beginning of the end for the Cheyenne, Arapaho, Ute, and other tribes who frequented the area.

Writing about this made me miserable, yet I had promised to write the truth, no matter how hard it would be for me. As I neared the deadline for my revisions, I worked all day verifying details and moving words here and there. The day flew by, and soon it was bedtime. I did not think I would make the deadline. I cried. "You can do it," said Mark, his voice kind and reassuring. "You just need to stay up and finish your book." So, I changed into my pajamas and sat back down at the computer. Mark and the kids hugged and kissed me goodnight and went to bed.

Then, in the quiet of the night, I gave Chipeta her voice through writing her story—one I hoped honored her.

At 2:00 a.m. on December 1, 2003, I printed the last page of my manuscript and laid it on the desk. Then I created a title page. I stared at the stack of paper and printed words that would be my book. I could hardly believe it was finally done and that I had undertaken such a project all because of a dream in 2000.

***The Storyteller.* Artwork by Vickie Leigh Krudwig. 2021**

Before I went to bed I did one last thing, I walked down to my studio and brought up a length of red satin ribbon and a small sage bundle. The ribbon was my acknowledgement of the Sacred Four Directions and the medicine wheel used by Indigenous tribes. As an artist and spiritual person, I loved the symbolism and power of the color red. It represented the east and spring and the re-awakening of the Earth (and the re-reawakening of myself) after a long sleep. It was the symbol of victory over winter, and it appropriately represented a renewed life, my life, given to me through writing *Searching for Chipeta*.

I lovingly tied the manuscript together with the ribbon and placed the sage bundle underneath it, to hold it in place. I had fulfilled my promise to Chipeta. I went to bed saying a silent prayer of gratitude to her and the Ancestors who led me to this moment in my life.

Chapter Eighteen
Ute Heritage Day

After I handed in the manuscript, I put my research materials into their binders and placed them on the shelves in my studio. I pulled out my watercolor paints, watercolor paper, pens, and ink and then started sketching the things I had seen in my dreams and visions. I also sketched what I had seen on my trips throughout Colorado, Utah, and parts of New Mexico. Then I did rough paintings of my very first Chipeta dream. One was of a mountain with a brook running down a slope. In it I placed an image of a woman flowing with the water down into a valley. Next, I did a painting of the window in the old building, with the blue and white dishes on a battered white countertop. Beyond the window, in the distance, were the People huddled together in the stark landscape.

I had already sketched in my journal the Ute Creation Story. I had shown the stick people running out of the bag Sinawaf had put them in until they finished becoming human. I loved that Coyote had opened the bag and let them out, and that they had run in all directions. Only a few stick people had stayed in the bag. Sinawaf scolded Coyote and then named the people in the bag Ute (Noochew). He placed them in the mountains where they would be close to the Creator.

The more images I created, the more I wanted to explore my creativity and art. If I could buy my own car, take a courage journey, and complete a book, I could take a college art class. The thought thrilled me, and I knew I had to act before I changed my mind. So, in January 2004, I signed up for a painting class at a community college. Under Polly's (Xio Chiang) instruction, I thrived in the class. I learned more about composition and still life drawing. I painted watercolor landscapes that captured the scenery of Montrose and the Uncompahgre Valley, and I painted meadows, mountains, teepees, and old stone tools.

I made art while I waited for the release of *Searching for Chipeta,* hoping my readers would receive it well. CJ had already scheduled a presentation and book signing for me at the museum for April 17. I thought about ways I could show my gratitude to Chipeta and the Ancestors, beyond my completing the book for them. I wanted a personal way to say thank you. I got an idea. I had seen news stories about people who had walked for causes and thought a walk might be a good way to acknowledge the Ute, their history, and their Colorado connection.

I told CJ I wanted to walk the ten miles from Montrose to Ouray in honor of the Ute People, as I saw myself making a pilgrimage to Ouray, the place where I had received the blessing. I knew it seemed a bit much, but it was a means of dramatizing the Ute's long march from Montrose to Utah. CJ recommended we stay in Montrose and walk along the pathway from Baldridge Park to the Ute Indian Museum, a mile-long stretch. This sounded perfect to me because I was in no shape to walk ten miles. Another show of gratitude was to proclaim April 17, 2004, Ute Heritage Day. I wrote a proclamation and sent it to Governor Bill Owens, who signed it and made it official. I kept this a secret until I knew the governor would approve it. In the meantime, CJ contacted tribal members and obtained their support for the walk.

Valorie wanted to accompany me to Montrose for my presentation. Of course, Mom was eager to go, too. Dad also wanted to visit Montrose, even though he was skeptical about the number of people who would show up for the walk. I was not sure what to expect, but I decided if it turned out I had to walk the route alone, I would.

Searching for Chipeta arrived at my home on April 9, a week before the walk. I held a copy up and looked at Chipeta's face on the cover. She gazed back at me, and my love for her surged through me. I inscribed and signed the first copy to Mark and gave it to him. I did the same for the kids. I also gave signed copies to my parents and in-laws. When my dad got his in the mail, he called to say it was beautiful. His words would mean more to me than he would ever know. He had recognized me as a writer. Roland and CJ thought the book was beautifully written. What a relief! I took books to the community college and signed one for my art teacher and let my classmates look at the others. I gave three or four classmates books and invited them to join me in Montrose.

Finally, Friday, April 16, arrived. I would drive to my parents' new home in Florence, Colorado, and spend the night with them. Then Valorie, who had recently moved to Pueblo West, would pick us up and drive us to Montrose. Excited, I could hardly contain myself. I was nervous, too. How would members of the Ute tribe and the newspapers receive my book?

Mark helped me load my t-shirts and two cartons of *Searching for Chipeta* into my car and kissed me goodbye. I had used the balance of my advance money from *Searching for Chipeta* to purchase one-hundred white silkscreened t-shirts bearing a pen-and-ink drawing I had created of Chipeta and the words "Walking to Remember." Mark kissed me, wished me well and told me to be safe. I got in the car and headed south to Florence. Once there, my parents and I chatted about my experiences, about the book, and about what to expect in Montrose. Valorie got there at 5:00 a.m. the next day, and we transferred suitcases, books, and t-shirts to her car.

I was anxious about getting to the walk on time, but I need not have worried. Valorie delivered us safely to

Baldridge Park in Montrose, just as CJ, Roland, and a large group of walkers, including many from the Ute tribes of Colorado and Utah, were gathering. My dad got out of the car and could hardly believe what he was seeing. "I had no idea," he said, hugging me. Then he wept.

Dad had been writing his own novel, *Boy Who Slept with Bears*, a story of a Ute boy who lived on the Southern Ute reservation in the late 1800s. He had started writing it when I was a young girl. I was not even aware of it until he began working on it in earnest—when I was working on the book *Searching for Chipeta*. We had had conversations about the spirituality of Indigenous people and the spiritual connections that happen when we are open to them. He had kept this part of himself tucked away for a long time.

As I shared more of my mystical experiences with Dad, he opened a little, and he had occasionally given me a glimpse of his true spiritual nature. The more we talked about the Ute and other tribes who had lived in Colorado, the more he talked about his own mystical experiences and spiritual connections to the Earth and history. We grew closer through these conversations.

My family put on their Walking to Remember t-shirts and then handed out shirts to Ute walkers: Ute Mountain Ute, Southern Ute, and Northern Ute. We handed out the balance of the shirts to other walkers. Everyone had a shirt on and there were none left! When it was time to start, CJ and Roland gathered everyone in a grassy area. We joined hands and stood in a circle. Roland lit a sage bundle and carried it around the circle, and we all washed ourselves in the sacred smoke. My dad, mom, sister, and I inhaled the aroma of burning sage while we pulled its smoke over our heads and down our bodies. I embraced the gift of the white tendrils of smoke as they wafted to the blue spring sky. Roland offered a prayer for Chipeta, Ouray, the Ancestors, their descendants, and for the non-Indigenous who had come to remember the People. I marveled at the sight of the Ute Elders, mothers, fathers, and children holding hands through the prayer.

Some of the Ute women wore their beautiful handmade shawls bearing vivid appliqués of geometrical shapes and flowers. Long, silky fringe bordered the shawls and swayed when the women walked or danced. It was a sight to behold. These moments felt surreal and frozen in time. I was humbled and grateful, and my eyes filled with tears. I picked up a large paper banner I had made, and CJ and Roland took hold, then we led the walk to the museum. Everyone moved as one along the path.

The morning was warm and sunny, and the pathway stretched through the meadows and along the Uncompahgre River. Globe willows were vivid green. Horses grazed on tender spring grasses in nearby pastures. I felt the spirit of the Ancestors and Chipeta walking with us. A reporter walked along and talked to me and the Ute walkers. Dad stopped now and then to take photographs and talk to walkers. I chatted with some people, and several Ute said they were glad the governor was honoring the Ute. "It's about time," said an elder woman from one of the Ute tribes. Her comment gave me such joy. After a while, I dropped back, to allow members of the Ute tribes to walk up front.

When we reached the museum, I took my place at the podium in the Chipeta Room, where a crowd had gathered. I spoke about the dream that started everything and about how I had felt while writing *Searching for Chipeta.* When I finished my talk, I signed copies of the book. My parents and Valorie watched for a while, then walked around the museum and the grounds.

After the program, I bid CJ and Roland farewell, and Valorie drove Dad, Mom, and me to Delta, to see the ancient Ute Council Tree. After that she drove us to Ouray, so Dad could see the places about which I had often talked. In the end, it had been a busy, but meaningful, day.

The next morning, Valorie drove us all to the lower Coal Creek Valley, to see John Inman, a long-time resident of Montrose. Mom and I met John in 2002, after being introduced to him by CJ. She recommended I visit him while I was in Montrose, and I did so. As a child, John had found the old stone pipe that I had mentioned to Roland and CJ, even though I had never seen it. I would see it for the first time April 2002. I was given a glimpse of the stone pipe at that time.

John Inman poses with the Colt pistol he found, along with stone pipe, when he was a young boy. **2003.**

CJ and Roland asked me to come by the museum in the morning before we headed back home. When we arrived at the museum, I parked in the museum parking lot. Mom said she would wait for me in the car. I followed CJ and Roland into the museum. They led me into a small room and shut the door. CJ pulled a small metal box out of a cabinet. Inside the box was the stone pipe, minus its wooden stem, that John found when he was young. With it was a handwritten letter from John Inman to the Ute Indian Museum. In it, John's own handwriting recounted the story of finding the pipe and an old Colt pistol in a hog wallow on his family's farm in the lower Coal Creek Valley. He was six years old in the early 1930s. He cleaned them up and kept them safe. A man from the Colorado Museum of Natural History in Denver (now the Denver Museum of Nature and Science) found out about the pipe and tried to buy it from him for $50—lots of money during the Depression. However, John's father told him if he sold the pipe, it and the money would soon be gone like a whisp of smoke. Because of this, John felt compelled to keep it.

When John was eleven, he became ill with severe appendicitis. He had surgery but developed a deadly infection. For over thirty days he lay in and out of consciousness. He woke once to find Ouray sitting in a rocking chair next to his bed. Ouray said to him, "You are the Keeper of the Pipe." Ouray revealed he was there to watch over John and keep the evil ones from taking over his body. He told John he would grow to be an old man, and that there would be a time when he would return the pipe to the People. John eventually recovered from his infection. He would keep the pipe with him and take it everywhere he went, including overseas when he served in WWII.

CJ gave me John's telephone number, so I called him right away. He invited Mom and me to go out to his home in the outskirts of Montrose. Since we were in Montrose, we decided we would go out to see him. When we arrived, John greeted us warmly. He was tall and slender and wore a chambray shirt and blue jeans that were dusty from his working in the fields near his home. I was intrigued by his story and told him I wanted to write a children's book about it. I took a photo of him holding the Colt pistol. We hit it off, and I quickly made friends with him and his sister and her family, who lived next door.

I would visit with John over the next year, and he would tell me more about his life experiences. He was an excellent storyteller, so while he talked, I took notes and recorded his words about his life. His parents had come to Montrose from Arkansas, to escape the Dust Bowl that had ravaged the land in the eastern plains in the 1930's. I told him that once *Searching for Chipeta* was complete, I would write his story.

Now, two years later, 2004, Valorie, my parents, and I drove together to John's place, a mobile home in the Coal Creek area near Montrose. Like he had with my mom and me in 2002, he showed us his photo albums from days gone by and the Colt gun he had found. We talked about Ouray and Chipeta and the lands on which John lived. He gave us flint pieces he had found on his property. His story enthralled my dad. John's family were kind and hard-working people who revered their land and its rich history. They had overcome many hardships to get to Colorado. When John was just three years old his family made their way west. They crossed the dust covered prairies and traveled through the Rocky Mountains in an old Model T Ford. His family, like many, through the Great Depression, would have many hardships along the way but persevered. John's story was certainly worth writing about.

While my parents and I were visiting John, I had him sign a contract I had prepared for the visit. It allowed me to use his photos and stories in the book. I had a new project to work on when I got home.

Val, Mom, and my Dad, just before we head home from Walking to Remember. 2004.

The morning after my family's visit with John, we all left for home. Once more, Valorie drove. We were a noisy group while we drove east on Highway 50. We had so much to talk about. Suddenly, the mood in the car was no longer celebratory, and everyone stopped talking. A spring snowstorm had shrouded the area east of Gunnison. The snow came down in big wet flakes and quickly made the road white and slippery. Valorie concentrated as she carefully made her way through the blowing snow and up the west side of Monarch Pass. The drive seemed to last forever. The higher we climbed, the harder the snow fell. The wind and poor visibility, along with slick roads, terrified us. I closed my eyes and prayed for safety. When we made it over the pass, into dry weather, and onto flat land, we all erupted in cheers and laughter. Luckily for us the rest of the drive to my parent's house was uneventful.

Valorie dropped Mom, Dad, and me off at my parents' house, where I stayed the night. On Monday morning we sipped coffee and talked about our amazing experiences we had over the weekend. This cemented my relationship with my dad, and with my mom, too. Dad was proud of me—and jealous, he later confessed. But we had found common ground in our love for Ute history. After our coffee and visit, I loaded my suitcases and remaining books into my car, kissed my parents' goodbye, and headed toward Denver.

The weekend could not have gone better. I would soon be doing school presentations about *Searching for Chipeta,* during which I would tell children and teachers the truth of what I had learned about Chipeta and the Ute people. I marveled at the road I had been on. I knew the journey was going to last awhile. Question was, was I ready for what was to come?

Chapter Nineteen

A Whole New Vision

By January 2005, my father had finished his manuscript, *Boy Who Slept with Bears*, and I had finished writing the book, *Keeper of the Pipe: A True Story of a Boy Called John and his Amazing Discovery of the Lost Ute Pipe*. I had also written and illustrated *We are the Noochew: A Brief History of the Ute and their Colorado Connection*, an interactive workbook (activities, cutouts, recommended historical sites, and more) to help Colorado teachers and students understand Ute history. Mark had helped me proofread the books. I had also hired someone to do the final proofreads before they went to press. I obtained a small business loan and registered my publishing company, Juniper Winds Press, with the state of Colorado. In early 2005, my publishing company had printed three books and placed them on the market.

Mom, Dad, Valorie, and I headed to Montrose on April 29, 2005, for the second Ute Heritage Day and the Walking to Remember event the following day. I had printed one hundred more t-shirts, in powder blue this time, and used the same design as in 2004 but added the new date. Over the weekend, Dad and John Inman would have book signings for their newly released books and I would have a signing for *We are the Noochew* and, of course, for *Searching for Chipeta*.

While I would love to say all book critics and reviewers had kind and positive things to say about *Searching for Chipeta*, I cannot. One woman wrote scathing reviews that made me cringe. She questioned my historical facts, which made me doubt my facts, even though I had done extensive research and had conversations with some of Chipeta's direct descendants. She questioned the way I wrote the book, so I then doubted my writing ability. I felt ashamed and fearful. She wrote her two reviews within months of each other. This was a bitter pill to swallow. So, I decided to find out who owned the magazine that had published her reviews. The reviewer turned out to be an author who had written a book about the Ute long before I had written *Searching for Chipeta.* I had her book on my bookshelf, which I considered ironic.

My new releases sold well, and within a short time my inventory ran low, so I needed to do a second printing. I was delighted to have such a great reaction to the books. Tattered Cover Book Store, Barnes and Noble, Amazon.com, Books West and other independently owned bookstores carried them. The Ute Indian Museum and Colorado History museums throughout the state also carried them.

By mid-summer, I had learned that all three of the books under Juniper Winds Press had won a 2005 CIPA EVVY (CIPA Education and Literacy Foundation Award) from the Colorado Independent Publishers Association. EVVY competition was a world-wide book publishing competition, with teachers, business leaders, authors, critics, readers, and others, as judges. Books were judged on overall content and quality. My new books, *We are the Noochew* earned a third-place award, *Boy Who Slept with Bears,* a first, and *Keeper of the Pipe,* an honorable mention. I was surprised and thrilled.

Mark and I attended the EVVY Awards celebration together. We dressed to the nines, sipped wine, ate delicious food, and relished the moment. Mark was now my best supporter, and I knew he was pleased for me. When the emcee announced my awards, I walked to the front of the ballroom and picked up a beautiful black glass plaque featuring the cover of the book with the name of the award etched in it. They were super fancy. When the emcee read the card for my third award, he said with an exaggerated sigh, "Vickie, *again*." The audience laughed and applauded. I carried the third award back to the table and set it next to the two others. Mark leaned over and told me he was proud of me.

Unbelievably, that summer my publisher told me *Searching for Chipeta* was the first-place winner in the children's category for the 2005 Mountains and Plains Booksellers Association Awards. Once again, Mark and I attended an award ceremony. We were thrilled to be there and see the book receive such an honor. Maybe this silenced the voice of the critic. I'll never know. I must say, I was tempted to send pictures of my awards to her, but I knew better. There will always be naysayers telling us what we cannot do, and critical people carrying around their own self-doubts and disappointments. I no longer needed anyone's approval to write.

Because of my EVVY awards, sales of my books were brisk. In a short amount of time, I had to reprint all three titles. My income was improving, I was booking presentations and book signings regularly. Everything seemed to be going well. However, in October 2005, I began seeing double and having distorted vision. I had been grocery shopping for my recently widowed father-in-law when the refrigerator cases in the store suddenly tilted and doubled. Then intense vertigo hit, so I grabbed on to my shopping cart. As soon as I was able, I drove myself home and called my doctor. I saw a neurologist who thought I could have had multiple sclerosis or a brain tumor. I flunked the neurological exam, but my MRIs and bloodwork were normal. I went to an eye specialist who prescribed prisms for my eyeglasses. This resolved the situation, though I still had terrible headaches, vertigo, balance issues, and nausea on a regular basis, especially when I was writing.

Every six months I had to get stronger prisms to relieve my double and distorted vision.

Despite these problems, I shared my Chipeta experiences with people who asked to hear about them and returned to my art class. Still fixated with capturing my thoughts and feelings through my artwork, I painted in earnest. In the fall of 2005, I registered for another art class, this one under the direction of Homare Ikeda, a wonderful instructor and a fine artist in his own right. He was kind about my artistic efforts. He encouraged me to meditate on my experiences before I picked up my brush to paint. This advice significantly changed my art *and* my life, because when I did this, every painting seemed to paint itself. I would feel energy coming from the mediums, canvases, and paper. I could not stop painting.

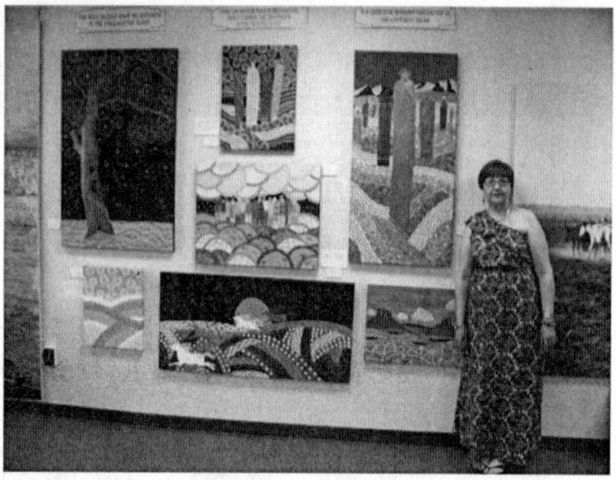

***My first exhibition at the Ute Indian Museum inside the Chipeta Room.* 2006.**

When the semester ended, I had finished a nice collection of colorful paintings. Images from Ute history and the rock art I saw while traveling populated my compositions. I sent CJ photos of my work, and in late 2005 she invited me to exhibit my artwork at the Ute Indian Museum in April 2006. We would have another Walking to Remember then, and she would invite guest speakers to come. I was nervous to share my art but thrilled at the prospect of having my first solo art exhibition at the museum.

Two days before the 2006 exhibit opened, I packed twenty-four paintings into my car, along with a few cases of *Searching for Chipeta; We are the Noochew;* and

Keeper of the Pipe. I barely had room for my luggage. I kissed Mark goodbye and headed south to Florence. I would spend the night with my parents, then Mom and I would head out early in the morning. On this trip, I would stop at a Gunnison elementary school to do an author talk about Chipeta and the Ute. I would also talk about how I wrote Chipeta's book.

To prepare for this visit, I spent months making and painting a leather storage pouch called a parfleche, like those I had seen in museums. I filled it with rabbit skins, sinew, scrapers, a small antler, a bison horn, shanks of colorful seed beads, and plastic animals representing the creatures important to the tribes for their food, clothing, and shelter. I also bought artificial cattails, real corn, and grains used to make food. I had even purchased from the Denver Museum of Nature and Science a framed display of native plants and their uses by the tribes.

I talked to kids about their backpacks and what they put in them, then I told them about parfleches. I talked about what life might have been like for the Ute people, and I showed them photos of Chipeta, Ouray, their homelands, and other historical sites. I told the kids the dark truth: The Ute had been forcibly removed from their homelands and pushed onto reservations. I told the young audience about my artwork in my car that would be displayed in the Chipeta Room in the Ute Indian Museum. I also told them about the Walking to Remember event.

At the end of the presentation, I played a flute CJ had given me. The kids quieted down as I nervously put my fingers on the blond beechwood flute and began playing. While the notes echoed in the gymnasium, I felt Chipeta standing behind me, and her energy mixed with mine, and my body tingled from head to toe. I hoped she was pleased. When I had finished playing, she whispered, "*The paintings in the dream were yours.*" For a moment, I was speechless. I had no clue about this. I had not given one thought to the art hanging in the gallery in that first dream. Now it made sense.

After I had signed lots of books for children and teachers, Mom and I quickly packed up the presentation material and the books and loaded them into my car. We were headed west to Montrose. I couldn't wait to get there. My paintings were going where they had belonged long before they were ever created. I felt Chipeta's spirit urging me forward. It was as if she were saying, "Hurry, we are waiting for you."

Once at the museum, Mom and I carried the artwork into the Chipeta Room and begin to unpack it. We visited with CJ and Bill, a docent at the museum, and then got to work hanging my artwork. After we finished this, Mom and I went back to our hotel to shower and change clothes before we returned to the museum to get ready for the opening reception for my exhibit. Roland would speak and then I would talk about my experiences while writing *Searching for Chipeta*. Then I would sign books for the museum.

That night, I stood in the Chipeta Room and watched people stand in front of my paintings and study them. I had written short essays for each one. The response to my exhibit overwhelmed me. People wept, others asked me questions, and still others said they felt emotion or energy emanating from the paintings. Several pieces sold. I was over the moon and grateful.

The following morning, April 26th, participants from the Ute tribes and the community at large met once again at Baldridge Park to walk to the museum. We all wore t-shirts of a new color I had had printed for the occasion. When we reached the museum, I participated in a round dance and listened to storytellers, flute music, and watched a short lesson on Indigenous sign language taught by CJ. At 1:00 p.m. I conducted my three-hour workshop, Preservation Through Print: Preserving Tribal History through Self-Publishing, which was well attended. The participants, including many members of the Ute tribes, were clearly interested in learning how to record their own histories through self-publishing.

CJ told me Lauren, a curator at the Telluride History Museum, had seen my exhibit in Montrose. Lauren had asked if I might want to hang the exhibit in the Telluride History Museum. Would I be interested in taking it there for the summer? “Yes! Of course!” I answered. Mark and I drove to Montrose to pick up the art on May 1st, then we drove it to the Telluride History Museum, and old Victorian building. Its wooden floors and a window displaying the majestic mountains in the distance reminded me of the first Chipeta dream. This further confirmed that I had seen my paintings in this dream.

Like in Montrose, the exhibit was well received. I sold more pieces, and I could hardly believe it. I was not done, though. I knew I would keep moving forward on this journey. I knew there was much more for me to experience and learn about the tribes and myself.

Utah’s Department of Education invited me to go to Salt Lake City on June 22, 2006, to talk to Indigenous educators about *We are the Noochew* and about why creating a new curriculum from a tribal perspective was important. I met educators from various tribes in the region who wanted to share their own histories and develop curriculum for their tribe’s children. They also asked me to present my Preservation Through Print workshop. My mom and I went there together. The Education Department had already purchased fifty books, which I had signed prior to my visit. Roland was there, and he spoke about his experiences growing up on the Uintah-Ouray Reservation and about Chipeta and the Meeker Incident. The room was quiet, and some people wept.

Later that summer, August 6th, Ben, and I drove to Blanding, Utah, where I was to present Preservation through Print to tribal educators in the southern parts of Utah. On the way, Ben told me I was going to have another spiritual experience, and I cringed. *Now what?* I wondered. He had the gift of intuitively knowing things, so I would have to stay aware and keep an open mind. The next day, I spoke to educators from the White Mesa Ute, Navajo, and Apache tribes, for whom I had created this custom workshop. I talked about writing curriculums and publishing their tribes' histories. I also shared what I knew about Chipeta and the Ute people. I felt Chipeta right behind me, reminding me to stand tall and proud. When I spoke, her words moved through me. My doubts about writing her history were replaced by confidence and a deep and meaningful connection to Chipeta and the Ancestors.

The program ended early in the afternoon. My host, a member of an Apache tribe in the region, had planned to visit a Medicine Man on the Navajo reservation. She asked if Ben and I would like to go with her and see ruins and petroglyphs along the way. We were thrilled she had asked. My host told me about a colleague from the Navaho nation, who would be our guide out there. He was one of the educators at the workshop, who wanted me to see the sites. He had said, "She will feel things there."

We climbed into our host's rented van and drove south of Blanding to a secluded place where we walked through an arid landscape to reach a rock outcropping. Just below it lay a hidden valley, green and thick with rabbitbrush and small trees, perhaps willows, following a creek bed. Our host pointed across the valley to a rock wall of a canyon, where there were barely visible ruins of ancient dwellings carved into the wall. It took my breath away. Oh, the stories those stone dwellings held. I felt the Ancestors' spirits in the ruins and down in the valley. I

Sand Island petroglyph sight was full of images made thousands of years ago by Indigenous people. **Photo courtesy of Benjamin Krudwig, 2006.**

shivered, knowing something important waited for us down the road. We stayed at the site for ten minutes and then headed south and then west on a narrow two-lane road.

Soon we were in Navajo country, the setting for many of Tony Hillerman's mystery novels. His stories centered around the Navajo and Hopi tribes in the American Southwest. I marveled at the vastness of the land and the rock formations jutting from the dusty, red earth. Our host pulled off the road to the Sand Island petroglyph site located along side a river. We saw a wall of rock art made eons ago by Indigenous artists for thousand years before the non-Indigenous people came. To prevent vandalism, a chain link fence had been installed to keep people from getting too close to it. The whole wall emanated an energy. The figures seemed alive and ready to jump off the rock. They would inform my later paintings. These images have become an integral part of my artwork.

August 8, 2006

We picked our way over to a bluff nestled amongst sage, juniper, and other dense brush. We climbed over some boulders and then we saw them, hundreds of petroglyphs carved into the rock wall: Kokopelli, birthing scenes, depictions of shamans, musicians, a cowboy (or a soldier) on a horse, spirals indicating direction or emergence, and more. I felt the presence of the Ancestors and their love of the land. I imagined them pressed against the red sandstone, scraping their existence (and history) into stone, I knew their lives were depicted in the incredible images before us. I was tongued tied by this. What I saw was beyond my wildest imagination.

From there, our guide had us follow him to the Medicine Man's house. We drove west for about twenty minutes. We left the highway and drove through red desert sand and across an arroyo. Ben and I held on for dear life as the van jerked up and down and swerved from side to side. I was certain we would get stuck. Our host seemed fearless! When we finally arrived at the Medicine Man's house, I thought we had landed in the middle of the desert.

Our host, Ben, and I waited in the car while our guide went into the house. When he came out, he invited our host to go in. After *she* came out, she said the Medicine Man wanted to meet me, so Ben and I went inside. The spiritual experience Ben had spoken of unfolded in spectacular manner. I choose not to go into detail about the encounter, but I will say it radically changed Ben's and my lives. Our thinking about the spiritual realm expanded. By then, both Ben and I had had too many mystical experiences to deny they existed.

Later that month, Mom, Ben, and I drove back to Montrose to take part in the annual Chipeta Day at the Ute Indian Museum. I was invited to come and sign books and help with the event. It was a busy day. Ute artists and other vendors set up in the Chipeta Room and outside on the patio. I had my first delicious fry bread filled with meat and other toppings, courtesy of the Ute tribes. Next, it was time for the dancers and drummers! I marveled at the dancers' traditional regalia in vibrant colors and at the striking shawls the women wore during the Fancy Shawl Dance. When the women danced to the drums and songs, they moved in a rhythmic way so that the fringe on their shawls would swing back and forth. In some Indigenous cultures, the Fancy Shawl Dance had its roots in the "Butterfly Dance." The shawl representing a cocoon when the butterfly emerges.

Willie, a magician, and storyteller performed while his wife, son, daughter-in-law watched. His infant grandchild was bundled in a beautiful cradleboard and moved me to think of Chipeta and the intricately beaded cradle boards she made for her family and friends. Willie and his family members of the Shoshone tribe.

Toward the end of the ceremony, Ute dancers invited everyone to join them in a friendship dance. Ute drummers raised their voices upward. Our feet moved in time over sacred grounds to the beat of Ute drums. Ben, Mom, and I all joined in and relished every second of it.

Chapter Twenty

Ancient Memories, New Voices

A year after *Searching for Chipeta* came out, I had the feeling that I had to get to the History Colorado Center immediately. I had planned for a lazy day at home in my art studio, but the voice in my head told me to go there NOW. I knew better than to ignore this voice, so I did as I was directed. Within twenty minutes of arriving at the museum library, a young Indigenous man walked through the doors. My heart thumped loudly as I watched him talk to the librarian. I was certain he was the reason I had come to the museum. I tried to focus on the computer screen in front of me to no avail. The man walked right over to my table, sat down, and sighed. He seemed overwhelmed by the vast number of materials and resources before him. I knew I must introduce myself. I was there to help him.

The young man's name was Funston Whiteman. He was Navajo and a member of the Southern Cheyenne tribe. He had lived most of his life in Oklahoma. He was passing through Denver on his way from Utah to Oklahoma. He had recently earned his master's degree in Educational Administration, following his getting a Bachelor of Science in teaching history. Funston said the Southern Arapaho and Southern Cheyenne tribes wanted to create their own history books for their children. (I knew this was related to the dream I had had in November 2003, in which Indigenous Ancestors from different tribes talked to me at the same time.) He had decided to visit the History Colorado Center library on the way home to Oklahoma.

He wanted to see what materials were available on his tribe's history. He only had two hours to spend there.

We talked about my work, and I shared my story about Chipeta and the first dream I had. I ran downstairs to the museum gift shop to buy a copy of *We are the Noochew.* Luckily, the shop had one left. I signed it and ran back upstairs. I handed it to Funston and told him that I was willing help the tribes if he would be interested in collaborating with me. Excited, he said he was eager to speak about this with the director of Tribal Education. He asked if I would be willing to go to Oklahoma to speak with the tribes. "Of course," I told him.

Driving home, I tried to grasp what had happened that morning. I was thrilled by this new ancestral connection and the possibility of another tribal project. I felt a familiar sense of the People. It was as if they had buckled themselves into the backseat of my car.

A week later, I received a call from Quinton Roman Nose, Director of Education for the Southern Arapaho and Southern Cheyenne tribes, in El Reno, Oklahoma. Quinton mentioned my conversation with Funston and then asked if I would be interested in going to Oklahoma to collaborate with the tribes. I said I was interested. I knew this was meant to be. He invited me to be a guest speaker at the 2005 National Indian Education Association in Denver in the fall. Quinton asked me to present my workshop, Preservation through Print, to more than one hundred Indigenous educators who had come from different tribal nations all over the United States.

In early October I made my presentation. The room was filled beyond capacity. People sat in the aisle, stood in the back of the room, and stood in the doorway. Meeting so many tribal members overwhelmed me. The stories they shared with each other and with me made it clear they wanted their voices and that of their Ancestors to be heard through a written history of their own. Tribal educators gave me their business cards and requested more workshop packets. Some said they would reach out to me. The seed was planted.

I did not hear from Quinton Roman Nose for a long time, and that was fine. The truth was, I was not ready for a meeting with the tribes so soon after writing Chipeta's story. I was not sure I was ready to face more of the burdens and blessings of helping the tribes write their histories. I instinctively knew the timing was not right for such a project.

As it turned out, I would eventually travel to Oklahoma in 2007, where I would meet descendants of Chief Black Kettle, Chief Roman Nose, Left Hand, Crazy Horse, and others who had made treaties with the government only to have the government break them. These descendants' Ancestors were brutally attacked on a cold and snowy morning in November 1864, during the Sand Creek Massacre. I knew I would have to face the horrors of this massacre plus those of the Washita and Wounded Knee massacres.

I had patiently waited nearly two years for the Southern Arapaho and Southern Cheyenne to formally invite me to meet with them in Oklahoma. In the meantime, I continued painting images from my experiences and doing school presentations through the state. Wherever I went, I felt Chipeta with me.

Chapter Twenty-One

Healing the Heart, Transforming the Spirit

Mom and I went to our third Walking to Remember and Ute Heritage Day in 2007 and, at the same time, hung my new exhibit, "Healing the Heart, Transforming the Spirit," in the Ute Indian Museum. My art was full of images from my dreams, prayers, and meditations. Once again, Roland, CJ, Bill, and my mother helped hang it while Indigenous flute music floated through the museum and mingled with cedar and sage incense. I was not as relaxed as I might have been, because within a few hours I would meet Chief Arvol Looking Horse and his wife, Paula, guest speakers at that night's art opening and at Walking to Remember.

Chief Arvol Looking Horse was the nineteenth generation Keeper of the Sacred White Buffalo Calf Pipe of the Lakota, Dakota, and Nakota Nation of the Sioux. From South Dakota, he and his wife traveled all over the world, promoting peace and prayer. They strived to connect with other Indigenous cultures and to promote preserving the traditional cultural and spiritual ways (tribal history) of the Lakota, Dakota, and Nakota people for future generations. To thank them for coming, I had planned to give them my painting, "The Last Buffalo." But then, at the last minute, a voice from within told me to give them "The Sacred Circle." This painting featured a female figure clad in white and gold paint in the center, the medicine wheel in the background, and, throughout the circle, creatures representing the two-legged beings (people), four-legged ones, winged creatures, swimmers, and crawlers.

The opening progressed nicely, even though I became increasingly nervous. Chief Arvol Looking Horse did not arrive until it was well underway and the Chipeta Room was full of people walking around and looking at my paintings. And then Chief Arvol Looking Horse and his wife, Paula were there. He had donned his full headdress and a buckskin shirt decorated with intricate beadwork, and she had worn a black floral dress and a beautiful, black-fringed shawl wrapped around her shoulders. As soon as everyone settled, Chief Looking Horse approached the podium and spoke passionately of Mother Earth and how she, as well as the People who live upon her, needed healing. He also spoke about The Sacred Circle and the White Buffalo Calf Woman. *I do not believe it!* I thought when I realized he was talking about images in my painting "The Sacred Circle." It filled my heart with joy and wonder.

The Sacred Circle presented to Chief Arvol Looking Horse and his wife, Paula Looking Horse. 2007.

When it was my turn to speak, I shared a bit about my experiences while writing about Chipeta's life and then about the artwork I had created based on these experiences. Then I presented my painting "The Sacred Circle" to them, and both their faces showed surprise. Paula said it had captured her eye the second she had walked into the room. Chief Looking Horse pointed out that the figure in the middle of the painting was White Buffalo Calf

Woman. Wow! This moved me. I was grateful for the guidance I had received about my choice of paintings.

Predawn the next morning, people who had been at the art opening gathered under a starry sky at the museum grounds to honor Chipeta and offer prayers for the People and the day ahead. Our teeth chattered from the cold as we stood in a circle in front of Chipeta's tomb and her brother's grave. CJ opened my large red wool bundle at the foot of the tomb, and someone smudged it, and everyone gathered with sage. No one uttered a word. The chilly morning air blended with the sage and holiness all around us.

Guided by a dream I had had in early January 2007, I had spent hours and hours, night after night over four months, cutting a rainbow of colorful fabrics into 2x2-inch squares, placing a pinch of fine tobacco on each square, and then tying them shut with colorful embroidery thread, creating prayer bundles. I prayed that all 6,500 of these bundles—one for every Ute man, woman, and child living on reservations in southern Colorado and northeastern Utah—would bless others. This was a gift to Chipeta, Ouray, and the Ancestors, to acknowledge the past, present, and the future. I put these small bundles on a large piece of red woolen fabric and rolled it up in tight bundle, which I tied shut with four different colored ribbons—red, yellow, black, and white—each representing The Four Directions and The Four Races. This was the bundle CJ opened at the tomb.

Speaking Lakota, Chief Arvol Looking Horse and his wife offered sunrise prayers to The Four Directions and then lit the sacred *Chanupa* (a Lakota name for the sacred ceremonial pipe). The pipe was carefully filled with tobacco, red willow, and kinnikinic. (There is a White Buffalo Calf Woman ceremonial pipe, but we did not use it because of its sacredness and power.) As a gesture of friendship and in honor of the day, we passed the pipe from person to person. When it was my turn to receive the pipe, I gingerly held it and drew in the pungent aroma of the tobacco mix, sacred smoke, and released it slowly. I offered silent prayers for safe and meaningful journeys for those who would come to walk later that morning.

Just as we had finished passing the pipe, the sun's rays touched the eastern horizon, setting the world ablaze with color. Chief Arvol Looking Horse and Paula began singing in Lakota. The ground was electrified with energy that went up and down my legs and up over the top of my head. I closed my eyes and offered my gratitude to Chipeta and the Ute Ancestors, and to the Indigenous Nations that had come before us.

After this prayer ceremony, CJ invited Mom and I to eat breakfast at the Uncompahgre Bed and Breakfast with Chief Arvol Looking Horse, Paula, Roland, CJ, and other members of the Friends of the Ute board. Before we ate, a tribal member offered a prayer was offered in gratitude for our meal, and then Paula made up a plate of food, an offering for the Ancestors, took it outside, and carefully set it on the ground.

During breakfast, I finally had the opportunity to talk with Chief Arvol Looking Horse and Paula. They thanked me for the painting and then asked if they could use it for the 2007 World Peace and Prayer Day poster. It would be used around the world, to encourage peace and unity among nations. I was honored and readily said yes.

This request was significant because in February 2004, before *Searching for Chipeta* was released, I had been speaking to Colorado educators about Chipeta and the Ute people, when an audience member, an Indigenous Central American, approached me and studied my face. Then, speaking softly, he said my work would go around the world. He asked me to open my hands. He pulled a flask of patchouli oil from his pocket, dribbled oil on my palm, and traced circles on my palm. Ben and I would later become friends with him and his wife.

When breakfast was over, we all went to Baldridge Park, the starting point for Walking to Remember. I had retrieved the red wool bundle and taken it with me to the park, as I had planned to carry during the walk, but a voice, Chipeta's, told me it was not my burden alone. She reminded me that everyone must help carry the bundle, as we all needed to take responsibility for carrying the Ute history into the future.

The bundle was passed from person to person during the Walking to Remember. Young and old alike helped carry it. **2007.**

Again, participants gathered in a large circle, and prayers were offered for the Ancestors, the Ute, and for everyone who had come to show their support and walk with us. I asked to speak and then shared Chipeta's instructions. The group thought taking turns carrying the bundle was a good idea. I started the walk by carrying it, and then, after three or so minutes, I passed it to a woman, who carried it and then passed it to her husband. And this went on until every member of the Ute tribe had carried the bundle—elders, men, women, teenagers, children, and even the young, though the bundle was as big as they were. Members of the surrounding communities helped carry the bundle too. With every step, I recalled the many lessons I had learned about the People, about their life and times, and about their struggles when non-Indigenous demanded more and more of their homelands.

After the walk, Mom went to the museum to sit down, and I strolled down the gravel path leading to Chipeta's tomb. I laid a personal prayer bundle at the tomb and at John McCook's grave. Chipeta and John were part of me, and I wanted to be part of them. I cried hard. Montrose and the grounds of the Ute Indian Museum had become my physical and spiritual home away from home. I was growing roots there, so I lamented going away.

The prayer bundles were smudged with sweet smelling sage. 2007.

I stood where I was and wept for the young children who were taken away from their loving families on the reservations and sent to non-Indigenous boarding schools. I wept because they were stripped of their heritage, their buckskin clothing burned or given away, their hair cut short (a sign of grieving in the tribes). I wept for the children who were sold for as little as $10.00 to non-Indigenous people who used them for labor. I wept for the countless men, women, and children who died of disease, starvation, and violence after they were forced onto the godforsaken reservations. I also wept for the ignorance of the non-Indigenous people who pushed the Ute and other Indigenous tribes out of their traditional homelands. I wept for Chipeta and Ouray, for their descendants, and for their children. I wept for Chief Arvol Looking Horse and his wife, Paula, and CJ, and for the Lakota, Dakota, and Nakota Nations and their losses.

Lastly, I wept for myself, for my disconnect with my own ancestral history, for the lost generations I had never learned about. I wept for my wasted years of fearful living, which kept me imprisoned in a self-made cocoon. I wept because I knew deep inside that I belonged in Montrose, where Chipeta was buried, and I could not stand the thought of living hundreds of miles away from the beloved San Juan Mountains and the meadows along the Uncompahgre. I wept until I had no more tears to weep. I left all my sorrows and part of my soul at Chipeta's tomb. I heard someone call my name, so I wiped my eyes and joined my friends in the green grass in front of the museum.

Chief Arvol Looking Horse spoke again. Spellbound, the crowd listened to him talk about life, the Sacred Circle, and about humanity and its future. My painting, Sacred Circle, was displayed on the stage. The people were moved by his words, and they nodded in agreement. Introspective and exhausted from the weekend, I compared my life before Chipeta to my life with her in it. I knew I had been blessed again and again, that my heart was slowly healing, and my spirit had been transformed. Deep down inside, I knew I could not stay there or leave the love of my life and my children. I had to face my life in Denver with the same determination I had used to write Chipeta's book. I could not and would not be a victim any longer.

My life would come full circle, like the Sacred Circle. I would go back to my home, my husband, my children, and to those who made my life both wonderful and unsettled. My journey toward home was a journey of the soul. It was time I decided which direction I would go and allowed myself to become whole and more authentic. It was time I left Montrose. It was time I left Chipeta's past behind and stepped into my own time and future.

Just before Chief Looking Horse concluded his talk, a female hummingbird flew overhead. *Another sign from Chipeta* I thought. My skin prickled. Chipeta was letting us know she was happy that we had come to honor her People. Also, she was letting me know I should embrace the pleasure in the journey ahead of me.

***CJ performs a song with sign language. My painting, Sacred Circle , is to her right. Walking to Remember.* 2007.**

Chapter Twenty-Two

Messenger from the Stars

Two years after I met Funston Whiteman, he called to let me know that the Southern Cheyenne and Southern Arapaho tribes in Oklahoma wanted me to speak to tribal leaders about my books and present a written proposal for the Cheyenne Arapaho Book Project. It would include four books for children kindergarten through sixth grade. I said I would, and agreed to visit them in El Reno, Oklahoma in early July 2007.

One morning after this, as was my custom, I sipped coffee and thought about the day ahead. On this day I thought about making a flight reservation and preparing my materials, and then I became apprehensive about taking on such a big project. Also, I still disliked traveling alone, especially out of state. Regardless of my worries, I booked my flight and notified the tribes of the details. Then I prayed a lot. I asked for guidance and protection while I traveled. I journaled, too, to sort out my thoughts and feelings. It helped me stay grounded.

During an early morning meditation and journaling, I contemplated whether I was supposed to collaborate with the Southern Cheyenne and Southern Arapaho tribes. Was I equipped to write such important histories? I was not sure I was physically, mentally, and spiritually up to the task. I had been connected to Chipeta's history and experiences, so much so that I had carried her heartache with me day after day for seven years. And yet, the dream of the Ancestors seemed so real, so real I could smell buckskin clothes when the Ancestors pressed towards me. I had said then that I would help them. But did they want me? The clock in the family room read 6:40 a.m. when a presence moved into the room and a great energy filled the space. *Who are you?* I wondered. *Why are you here?*

The presence was neither male nor female. Its message came through clearly and without hesitation. I wrote the words in my journal as they came. If I tried to change the grammar or words, the voice stopped and waited patiently for me to write each word exactly as spoken.

June 16, 2007

***Messenger from the Stars.* Artwork by Vickie Leigh Krudwig. 2021.**

I am of the Earth, Sky, and the Waters, said the voice. *I am the beginning of the People, and I am the end of their journey. I walk among them, close to their sides to keep them moving in a good direction. I am the warrior who hunted on the vast open plains, and I am the sacredness of the woman, who brought life into this world. I am the child who asks questions in a thirst for knowledge of the Ancestors. I am a soul that has seen many lifetimes, witnessing the many facets of humanity. I have lived and breathed the Indian way of life, and I wait again to come back to the People.*

I am keeper of sacred dreams and knowledge. I am the memories of all who have walked the sacred Earth long before you. I am the feminine and life-giving waters of rivers and seas. I am the mountains and valleys formed by the Creator himself. I am the stars and the planets that light your way into the dreamtime. I am the traveler who comes in early dawn to send you visions, to whisper urgent messages of remembering who we were.

I am the voice of millions of Ancestors who weep at the losses long ago. I am hope for the future when we return to the old ways, when our children will know and grow from our history. I am of every particle in the Universe... my bones no longer house my soul. Yet, I linger to help bring about the healing of hearts and minds, and to guide and protect you. I will provide you with understanding of what is to be.

I light the sacred pipe, which you smell. It is a gift and a blessing. It is protection, it is in friendship, that we may all walk in the beauty of what was—the old ways, and into the future. Like a hummingbird, you will travel in many directions to help heal the past, present, and the future. Listen to the Earth and her messages. Paint, write, and remember! I am part of you, and you are part of me, and part of something sacred. Lift each day in prayer. Watch for signs and messengers. They are all around you. All that you need will be provided.

These were the words I needed to hear. I had been called by a force greater than myself, and I knew that I must not fail when I helped the Southern Cheyenne and Southern Arapaho tribes of Oklahoma write their histories. I realized, as I had with Chipeta's story, that I had to commit my entire being to the cause and put my beliefs into action, whether I was ready for it or not. In July 2007, I presented my proposal to the Southern Cheyenne and Southern Arapaho Tribal Legislature for consideration. It reminded me of the television series, West Wing, only an Indigenous version. We had last minute adjustments to the proposals, and copies to make, before I presented the materials to the leadership. I spoke to the tribes, told them about my Chipeta experiences, and about the dream of the Ancestors. I looked them in the eyes and told them I had come to acknowledge the atrocities the tribes suffered at the hands of non-Indigenous. I was there to help the tribes tell their own stories. Both tribes voted unanimously to fund the project.

Within the next year, the Cheyenne Arapaho Book Project was well underway. I would coordinate the project, oversee, and assist with the writing and illustrations, hire editors, design the books, and work with the printers. We hired Southern Cheyenne and Southern Arapaho writers and illustrators for all four books. Funston Whiteman was the project director, Michael Bell (a native of Guam, an Indigenous education advocate, and assistant for our project), Funston, and I would write *The Tsististas Journey: An Introduction to Cheyenne History,* for children, grades preschool through second grade, and *The Tsististas: People of the Plains,* for third through sixth grade. Cover and interior artwork for these books would be created by George Levi, a Southern Cheyenne, who was a talented and well-known artist, and Vernon Bullcoming created the painting for our book cover. George would create drawings like the ledger art his Ancestors produced more than a century ago. I would manage the simple line drawings for all the books.

The Arapaho books, *The Hinono'ei Way of Life: An Introduction to Arapaho History*, would be for preschool through second grade, and *The Prairie Thunder People: A Brief History of the Hinono'ei* would be for third through sixth grade. Frank Mosqueda, a Southern Arapaho, and I would co-write both books, and Michael Bell would assist us on *The Prairie Thunder People* book.

Both book covers and interiors would be illustrated by the talented, well-known artist Brent Learned, a Southern Arapaho. Again, I would contribute the simple line drawings. Michael Bell would assist with these books as well.

During our project, our whole group traveled around Oklahoma to gather materials and listen to elders share their wisdom and stories passed down from previous generations. At these gatherings I would meet descendants of Chief Roman Nose, Black Kettle, and others whose way of life was drastically and tragically altered because of the Sand Creek Massacre in November 1864. The Cheyenne and Arapaho had agreed to live along Sand Creek and no longer fight the white man. Ignoring this agreement, Colonel John Chivington ordered a predawn surprise attack on their camp, when hundreds of men, women, and children were asleep in their teepees. His troops fired cannons and a howitzer gun. Panic ensued, and the people ran for their lives. My stomach churned as I heard the horrific and inhuman details of the attack directly from the descendants of Black Kettle and others.

Black Kettle waved the American flag given to him by the United States government. He also raised a white flag of surrender over his teepee, but the troops continued their massacre anyway. Trying to hide from the soldiers, women and children dug into the ice encrusted banks of Sand Creek. They could not hide, though, and hundreds of them, along with tribal elders, were slaughtered. (Black Kettle would experience another massacre in 1868, the Washita Massacre, led by Colonel George Armstrong Custer.)

Just after the Sand Creek Massacre, Chivington and his soldiers rode to southwest Colorado near Conejos and showed off their howitzer gun to the Ute tribes living there. Hearing this disgusted me. In other words, Chivington had planted the evil seed of what could happen to the Ute, too, if they did not sign the latest treaties. How this outlandish demonstration must have terrified Chipeta and the Ute people. They only wanted peace.

I tried to listen openly as the Elders related the tragic stories passed down from one generation to another. I felt their Ancestors' pain and anger, and it seemed as fresh in 2007 as it was that snowy morning in 1864. When I was tempted to turn away, I did not. I could not turn my back on the tribes, as I had made a sacred contract with the Ancestors. It was important for me to listen to their tragic stories and to *acknowledge* the ugly side of history and the pain they still felt generations later.

At a luncheon held as part of an interview gathering, an elder Chief offered a prayer for the luncheon, and his voice carried me across the threshold of time. His traditional language transcended time and space, and, for a moment, I felt the presence of the long-gone Ancestors. I unsuccessfully gulped down my emotions, and, instead, sobbed uncontrollably and could not look people in the eye. There were men, women, and children in attendance who, like me, fiercely loved their families. Their sorrowful expressions broke me. I ran outside. An older woman came out and patted me on the back. She bid me to come back into the room. It was time to hear the rest of the stories the Elders had to share. I knew it was crucial that their voices be heard.

Though the topics were difficult, there was still laughter and friendship. Each time we gathered, the Arapaho and Cheyenne people generously provided meals and showed kind hospitality. They also generously shared their knowledge of their cultural and traditional ways, making it possible to produce four beautiful books for the children of the tribes.

During this time, I again lived in two distinct worlds. I found comfort in the customs, traditions, and spiritual beliefs of the Southern Cheyenne and Southern Arapaho.

As time went by, I saw my world through the eyes of the Ancestors and their descendants. The land my house sat on was no longer part of a municipality, but part of traditional lands once traversed by the Arapaho, Cheyenne, Lakota, the Ute, and many other visiting tribes.

I would be dishonest if I said all my conversations with tribal members were wonderful and full of wisdom. Sometimes my culture, race, and gender clashed with the tribe's customs and beliefs. With each new meeting with Elders came a mix of emotions on both sides. For the first time in my life, I was a minority. I sat in meetings in which "white" had a negative meaning. Whenever tribal members talked about "the white man" I felt deeply ashamed and sad.

Still, I could not run away from the atrocities meted out by non-Indigenous people. I could not run away from my own culture and history either. I desperately wanted unconditional acceptance from the tribes' men and women, and I wanted the tribes to adopt me. When I was in the People's presence, I forgot that I was a white woman. When the drums played and songs and prayers were offered up to the Creator, I felt alive in ways I could not describe. I soared with joy and a sense of connection to the spiritual and natural world, and I was finally beginning to feel whole and at peace.

I had to gather my courage and stand tall in front of the Southern Cheyenne, Southern Arapaho—and the Ute—tribal members and acknowledge their sorrow and resentment. *Maybe this is my purpose* I thought. *I must look into the eyes of the descendants whose lives were forever affected by the winds of change, and honor their need to express their grief and, yes, outrage.* I did not turn away from the people. I listened to them, and I wept with them. When I spoke about the project, I told the Tribal Council about Chipeta and the dream I had. It felt important to tell them. They acknowledged my dream and the journey I made to write her story. Now, I had come to acknowledge their history, and to help them record it for future generations.

As with any large project, there were occasional disagreements while planning and writing the books. Sometimes our cultural differences discouraged me. I was in Oklahoma for ten days. I was alone, away from home, scared, and I felt like an outsider. One of my sisters suggested I quit and come home. It sounded like the easiest thing to do. I would repeatedly remind myself to put aside my ego and put the future of the children of the tribes first. I needed to trust in my own abilities to help the tribes get the job done and, more important, while taking care of myself and my needs. The Tribal Council voted unanimously to hire me for the project. It seemed they trusted me, as my previous work spoke for itself. This was an opportunity to learn how to be independent and on my own and, and when necessary, speak up for myself. Not an easy thing for me. I also refused to break my agreement with the tribes.

I began longing for connection to my own Ancestors. I was not even sure where they had come from, except Norway, Scotland, Sweden, and parts of Ireland. I started reading historical documents that my Great Aunt Elizabeth had sent to my father decades earlier, but I had never bothered to read through them. Before she died, Aunt Elizabeth and I had talked over the phone about our family's history on my father's side. She told me that her mother, Fannie, my great, great grandmother, born in Yankton, South Dakota, in 1874, was part Indigenous. I had no way to validate this. I had wanted desperately to have a connection to the tribes in the northern Great Lakes region or the Dakotas, so I had searched documents and census records for my family's surname. Oddly enough, it appeared in the Quapaw tribe in Oklahoma, but Fannie's name was nowhere to be seen. She never discussed her parents or her past. Her mother, Amanda, was born in Ontario, Canada, in the 1840s and had moved into Dakota

Territory with her husband, Fred, to take advantage of the land grants.

Fannie's father, my great, great grandfather, Fred, served as sheriff in Yankton, South Dakota, from 1879 to 1881. This was a tumultuous time for many of the tribes I was working with, and well-known Indigenous leaders were jailed then. I could hardly stand the thought of my great, great grandfather playing such a role in American history. I had no words for how I felt about him.

There were days when I wanted to walk away from the ugliness of the history I was writing. It hurt me to see in black and white the reality of the lives of the Southern Cheyenne and Southern Arapaho. In the darkness of night, I would sometimes cower under my covers. Then I would wake up dreading another day of writing about the pain and suffering of the people.

When the going got tough, I would think of the Ute, Cheyenne, Arapaho, and thousands of other Indigenous tribes who had persevered through the harshest of times. My problems were nothing compared to theirs. I had to become strong inside and out, and face the facts shared with me. I began to think of myself as a warrior woman: a woman with courage, love for humanity, and the desire to help others heal. I had a mission. I constantly prayed for guidance in connecting the past to the present. I moved forward without looking back. I did not want to fail in our quest. Although I was scared, the words I had journaled that early morning in June always comforted me.

It was during this time my vision problems returned with a vengeance. I would work on the manuscripts, then lie down on my office floor and wait for the vertigo and nausea to go away. I had more headaches and double and distorted vision. Still, I pressed on. I had to. While I wrote *Searching for Chipeta*, I learned Chipeta had cataract surgery in her later years. It must have been painful for her, given the dry and dusty conditions in the early 1900s in eastern Utah. Sadly, her surgery was unsuccessful, and she would eventually become blind.

In late August 2008, my company, Juniper Winds Press, helped the tribes produce all four of their books, *The Tsististas Journey: An Introduction to Cheyenne History*; *The Tsististas: People of the Plains*; *The Hinono'ei Way of Life: An Introduction to Arapaho History*; and *The Prairie Thunder People: A Brief History of the Hinono'ei*. In addition to co-authoring and illustrating the books, I designed the books and set them up for press, I also communicated with printers and sent proofs back and forth to Oklahoma for approval. The Cheyenne Arapaho Book Project had been one of the most difficult projects I had ever worked on. It had required numerous tribal meetings, interviews, and lots of research to pull our resources together. Despite some setbacks we (my co-authors, co-illustrators, and I) managed to successfully meet our publishing deadline. In September 2008, the Southern Cheyenne and Southern Arapaho tribes of Oklahoma became official publishers of their own written histories. I was thrilled later to see photos of Southern Cheyenne and Southern Arapaho children holding books containing their ancestral history.

Finishing this project did not mean I had finished thinking about the tribes. I was still fixated with the history of the Ute, Cheyenne, Arapaho, Lakota, and other tribes. I would talk about their history and recommended their books to anyone who would listen. I would speak to groups of adults and children about writing *Searching for Chipeta* and the experiences I had. Overall, most people were receptive to what I would tell them. Sometimes audience members walked out of my presentations, disgruntled about the way the People had been treated. People cried. One man, an attorney, told me he was sick and tired of hearing about the tribes and their hardships. Another man told me there was no evidence that the Ute had lived in the mountains near Telluride. I had to remind him that the People left little behind—unlike the miners who had mutilated and trashed the land.

Perhaps it was easier for people to deny this painful part of our history and the hardships endured by the tribes. Whatever the explanation, I could not let a few people keep me from moving forward in this sacred journey. Whenever I closed my eyes and listened to the ancient prayer songs of my Indigenous friends, I could feel the energy of the Earth rise through my being, connecting me to a world of Spirit, where all things are interconnected. I would think about my future. What would happen next? Would I write more books with other tribes? Would there be other projects? I could not say.

Somewhere along my journey, my fear of death, which had paralyzed me and kept me anxious, had diminished. My Cheyenne co-author told me that the tribes believed the stars in the Milky Way were their Ancestors who had died a long time ago. They stayed up there, he said, to watch over the People below. He also told me that we were all made of stardust and will return to the stars when we die.

***Blessed are the Peace Makers.* Artwork by Vickie Leigh Krudwig, 2022.**

Starry skies became a big part of my artwork. I wanted to capture the cosmic connection we have to the earth, water, and sky. When I create art, I am walking amid the stars and planets with the Ancestors.

The petroglyph-like figures in my artwork were inspired by my experiences looking at rock art on the walls of red sandstone canyons in the southwest and feeling a definite energy emanating from them. Whether it appeared as rock art, petroglyphs, pictographs, ledger art, or winter counts, the message was clear: we all are part of something big and beautiful.

Traveling at the Speed of Light. **Artwork by Vickie Leigh Krudwig. 2022.**

Chapter Twenty-Three

Walking Two Roads

In 2010, I was sitting in an art class, studying 3-D art forms. The class had created story boxes about our lives. I was really into it and had filled mine with family names and photos, with twigs from the Delta Council Tree, and with pebbles and feathers. I had placed a bird's nest inside, and inside that, a picture of me as a little girl, asleep on my side. The box was deeply personal, as though it held my entire past.

***My life was summarized inside the assemblage project.* Artwork by**

Our instructor, Lydia, asked us to talk about our boxes, so I began by talking about the dream I had about Chipeta and my experiences writing her story. All the sudden I blurted out, "The little girl in the nest reminds me I have been asleep for the last thirty years of my life." I began sobbing. The room grew quiet, and Lydia quickly scooted our attention to the next student. I spent the rest of the class thinking about what I had said.

I was wide awake by then, and my life brimmed with possibility. I had gone from a frightened and tranquilized girl to a woman with a new awareness of the world. I had gone from terrified and unfulfilled to a fulfilled artist, writer, and, as my Indigenous friends said, a "Dreamer, Communicator, and Healer." Sometimes my Southern

Cheyenne and Southern Arapaho book partners referred to me as *Warrior Woman* because I was stern about meeting deadlines. As Funston once put it during a meeting with tribal members, "We have to call her Warrior Woman because Stands with a Fist was taken." When he said that, the room erupted in laughter, as the reference to the movie Dances with Wolves was not lost. I felt honored to get such a title. It is still my archetype when I am facing life's challenges.

I attended Indigenous events in Denver as well as volunteered at the AlterNative Voices public radio station for a while. As I met more tribal members, I remembered the dream with the Ancestors in 2003, in which I walked with different tribes, each speaking their own language. The dream had led me to a future I could not have imagined. How many times do we humans ignore the call of the soul?

Early in my experience with Chipeta, I had felt the overwhelming need to save the tribes and yet I came to understand two decades later that they did not need me to save them. They were strong and had their old ways and traditions to guide them into the future. I had to let go of the notion of rescuing them and, instead, focus inward. I could not judge others for the paths they were on. I know that the road I walked had to be walked alone, and in the lonely moments I had to listen to my heart and intuition with everything I had. I knew I needed trust in my ability to find my way.

Whenever I was paralyzed by fear, I would remember Chipeta's words, her struggles, and her courage to overcome almost impossible obstacles. There were times when I would wrestle with what my life had become. I had had untold moments of alienation from friends and family members who could not understand my fixation with Chipeta, the Lakota, the Ute, the Cheyenne, and the Arapaho. Sometimes I grew angry and impatient because some

So Shall It Be. **Artwork by Vickie Leigh Krudwig, 2022.**

non-Indigenous people did not seem to care about the tribes. I wanted them to walk with me on this journey.

I struggled over the last twenty years, but Chipeta's words always arrived at the perfect time. The dream of the Ancestors would comfort me and provide inspiration to embrace change and trust that my life was unfolding as it was meant to. They still hold power today.

Chipeta taught me to "love simply, and simply love others." She also taught me about perseverance, which altered how I perceived the world. I still get angry about political issues, the loss of sacred lands to developers, violence, and now the Coronavirus pandemic. I grieve losing healthy vision, my changing body, and loved ones who have passed away. But I am grateful for my life and know I can persevere like Chipeta.

Chipeta's words are written in ink on the pages of my journals. They remind me that all individuals have a purpose and place in the world, and that includes a fearful forty-three-year-old woman who would discover the hidden strengths within her being. Our souls know what we need when we need it. They connect us to the spiritual realm and guide us into a fruitful and meaningful life if we listen.

Chapter Twenty-Four
Letting Go

On a Friday in May, 2010, I traveled alone to Ouray, Colorado, to pay homage to Ouray and Chipeta. The Ouray County Museum and History Society would be unveiling a bronze of Chief Ouray, sculpted by Jim Opdahl. I had been invited to attend the event which would be held the following morning. On Friday night, I watched Roland speak to a large audience about his Ancestors and about the significance of the vapor caves in Wiesbaden Spa. I remembered his and my conversation at the top of the hill above the spa in 2002 and smiled. I was celebrating the recognition of Chief Ouray and Chipeta, and the Ute who called the region home. It was Chipeta, and writing her story, that helped me find my voice and place in the world.

After Roland's talk, CJ, Roland, and I walked under a misty night sky to the spa. I was given a cozy room in the main building, just above the vapor caves. The floor was naturally warm, so all was snug and cozy. Looking around, I wondered if I would feel Chipeta's presence again. I changed into my swimsuit and met CJ and Roland in the heated, outdoor mineral water pool. Members of the Southern and Ute Mountain Ute tribes were already soaking there. A gentle rain fell, and I marveled at the simplicity of the moment. The rain made everything feel fresh and clean, and it smelled wonderful. Though chilly, I felt invigorated and very much alive.

We all stayed in the pool awhile and then went down to the vapor caves, where we sat in silent contemplation under the dome of the dimly lit cave. I felt at home there, peaceful, and whole. I felt embraced by Mother Earth, her warm waters soothing my tired body and mind. My love swelled then, for Mark, my family, friends, and, yes, even for my home in Denver. I prayed for them all. I also prayed for CJ, Roland, their families, my Ute, Cheyenne and Arapaho friends and their families, and for Indigenous people everywhere. I thought of all the amazing people I had met and the spiritual lessons they had shared with me. I was filled with gratitude for the life I had lived in the prior ten years.

***Chief Ouray bust at the Ouray County Museum.* Created by sculptor Jim Opdahl. 2010.**

After we had soaked a long time, we stood in a circle and Roland sang a prayer. I could hardly contain myself, as I wanted to lift my voice in song, too. I did not, however, as I was too shy. We offered our prayers and gratitude to those who had lived before us.

As I lay in my bed later, thinking about that little white house behind the spa, I pictured Chipeta and Ouray asleep in their adobe home while stars filled the night sky. I pictured them sleeping while it rained, the granite and sandstone cliffs standing guard.

Rain showers and rivulets of water running down my windows greeted me the next morning. Fortunately, the rain stopped long enough for the Ute dignitaries, CJ and Roland, both dressed in their regalia, to speak to the group gathered in front of the Ouray County Museum and Historical Society for the unveiling ceremony. Next, CJ and

Roland unveiled the bronze bust of Chief Ouray. Shortly after the ceremony a soft gentle drizzle fell from the gray skies. Droplets trickled down Ouray's cheeks, representing, I believe, the tears generations of the People had shed over the losses the Ute had endured.

After the ceremony, I helped CJ present Indigenous activities and games for adults and children inside the Ouray County Museum. When the event at the Ouray County Museum was over, I went back to the Wiesbaden Caves and Spa to soak in the hot springs inside the caves. CJ and Roland left to perform a wedding ceremony somewhere in Ouray. I settled in my room, where I was content to write in my journal and read. I was learning to savor solitude, a gift to cherish. It was in this stillness that I always learned the most about myself and received precious guidance.

On Sunday morning, Roland and CJ joined me in the sacred vapor caves one more time before I set out for Denver. As usual, I dreaded leaving the contentment I felt in Ouray and Montrose and the Uncompahgre Valley. Like I had the day before, I prayed silently. Then I stood and joined hands in friendship with Roland and CJ, to offer a prayer of gratitude to the Creator and the Ancestors. Once more, Roland's voice echoed off the cave walls. Overflowing with love for Chipeta and her people, I sang along. Then I heard Chipeta tenderly and lovingly whisper, "*It is time to let go. Your work on my behalf is done.*" Her nudge was gentle but firm, and I knew she was right. I bid CJ and Roland farewell, then I left the cave. I dressed in silence, knowing this was a holy moment for me.

I put my suitcases in the car and drove toward Montrose. The drive through Ridgway and down through the canyon was a bittersweet ending to my ten-year journey. I was going home to Westminster where my heart was, with my husband and children, family, and friends. Home was also a place within me. I could embrace the gifts of all my experiences collaborating with the tribes. I accepted that I did not need to belong to a particular tribe to feel connected to the Ancestors. My connection to Chipeta, the Ute people, the Ancestors, and my other Indigenous friends I made would last me all my life.

My eyesight was still changing, and yet I truly saw the world in a whole new way. I viewed it from the place of my soul. I would find more ways to express it through my artwork. I would explore Reiki and, employing the energies and principles of the chakra colors in my artwork. The bright colors provided more contrast for my eyes when I worked on my canvases. Intrigued, I took classes in Reiki and eventually became a Reiki Master.

Now it was time for me to embrace my own life and future. I marveled as I drove down the highway toward home. I had walked two distinct roads, both leading me to a sacred place where I was connected to the dream time, past and present, to Indigenous cultures, and to my own Ancestors. "Thank you, Grandmother," I whispered. My heart was full of joy and gratitude.

Chapter Twenty-Five

Courage, Compassion, Inspired

In early 2018, I received a call from Georgina Owen, Title VI Coordinator for Culturally and Linguistically Diverse Education, with the Colorado Department of Education. She informed me that the Ute Mountain Ute and Southern Ute tribes of Colorado, along with the Colorado Department of Education, Colorado Commission on Indian Affairs, History Colorado, Ute Indian Museum, Colorado teachers, and other collaborators were in the process of producing the curriculum *Nuu~Ciu Strong: Lessons about the Ute People of Colorado, A Colorado Fourth Grade Resource Guide:* She wanted to know if parts of *We are the Noochew: A Brief History of the Ute People in Colorado*, could be incorporated into their curriculum. She said the educational materials would be developed around the Ute tribe's history, to help teachers and students better understand the Colorado Ute tribes. "Yes, you can use them!" I said, honored she had asked me.

Right then and there, I decided to transfer all rights for *We are the Noochew* to the Ute tribes of Colorado and Utah. I contacted my intellectual property attorney and had him create a legal document that allowed me to transfer to the tribes all rights to any materials that I had produced for this book: the workbook *We are the Noochew*, the activities from the book, and the blackline master sheets used by teachers to make copies for students. Then I sent letters to the tribes telling them what I'd done, and I included DVDs and thumb drives of all my materials.

Then I boxed up everything to deliver to Georgina at the Colorado Department of Education, where the tribes and their collaborators would meet. Mark was kind enough to deliver the materials to their intended destination. I felt jubilant and thrilled to be part of such a significant project.

In May, I received both a lovely letter and an email from the Ute tribal headquarters, inviting me and all the collaborators of the project, *Nuu~Ciu Strong* to a luncheon to celebrate the completion of the project. The email included a link for the new curriculum. I opened it and my heart swelled! The Nuu~Ciu Strong materials were well written and wonderfully rich in Ute culture, traditions, and its long, long history in Colorado. At the bottom of the list of acknowledgements was my name, Vickie Leigh Krudwig. My journey with Chipeta and her Ute Ancestors had come full circle. Sadly, I was unable to attend the luncheon, due to my vision difficulties and my position as Resident Life Director at a senior retirement community.

In December 2019, I took a leave of absence from this position because my vision was worsening, and I needed to rest my eyes and get injections to alleviate the pain in my eye muscles. I had already had two major eye muscle surgeries that only made my vision worse. Injections were a last attempt to alleviate my symptoms. Unfortunately, they were painful and ineffective, so I had to permanently block my right eye to have singular vision. I would formally resign my position in March 2020, as I was no longer able to read well or perform my daily tasks without difficulty.

In January 2020, the Coronavirus pandemic reared its ugly head, transforming the world as we all knew it. Like most people, members of my immediate and extended family struggled with protecting themselves, and others, using masks and isolation. Family members struggled with anxiety and the uncertainty caused by this deadly disease. Out of necessity, our families couldn't be together, which made my life feel out of control. I'd lie in bed at night, filled with dread and unable to sleep. I couldn't bear to see my family and friends suffering.

My son, Ben, moved away from Colorado a month before the pandemic really took hold of the United States, in February 2020. He'd separated from his wife of six years. She would move to Germany, and he would move to Los Angeles, California. This happened on short notice, and I was in disbelief. I missed my son but knew I could not keep him from his own life's journey.

On April 27, 2020, after twenty-seven days on a ventilator, my dear friend of 24 years, Frank Lloyd Kramer, died of Covid-19. He and I had worked on two children's poetry books together, and he had read an early draft of this book. He encouraged me to move forward on it, adding that my book would be about writing *Searching for Chipeta,* about walking through her history while at the same time walking through my own self-discovery. Frank was not only my friend but also my mentor. I will never get over losing my dear friend and creative collaborator.

***My new art studio is filled with paintings and the energy of the Ancestors.* Artwork by Vickie Leigh Krudwig. 2021.**

As Covid-19 continued to ravage the world, I stayed home and created artwork at the kitchen table. Mark and I hired a construction company to finish our basement. By August 2020, I moved into a bright new art studio in our finished basement. Mark had helped me design the work area to help maximize visibility while I worked. Side by side, we painted the walls, picked out the cabinets and countertops, and created a loving and peaceful working space. Since then, I have covered the walls with paintings I have developed from images drawn in two decades' worth of journals. A small altar sits in a corner; it is filled with stones, twigs, feathers, and a fountain. The gentle sound of the fountain reminds me of the mountain brook I heard in my first dream about Chipeta. These mementos are reminders of the incredible life I have led over the last twenty years.

A 1913 photo of Chipeta and the Ute People that Roland gave me, hangs above a door. It commemorates one of the last gatherings of the tribe in the Garden of the Gods in Colorado Springs—a place where I had played as a child. Nearly blind in this photo, Chipeta was surrounded by her family and tribal members. She would continue doing her amazing beadwork, using carefully arranged containers of colorful beads and a helper to guide her to the colors. I keep this photo, along with a photo of CJ, Roland, and I, taken on the night we first met, in a place where I can see them every day to remind me of the blessings I've received.

Unable to travel or spend much time outside because of Covid and wildfires, I spent my days inside working on art and resting my eyes. Making art kept me focused and in a more peaceful place. I continued to create dot paintings, which became prayer paintings, filled with the loving energy of long-gone Ancestors. I felt their presence as I worked. When I retreated into prayerful contemplation before picking up my paintbrush, my work painted itself. I also painted greeting cards and sent them to my loved ones. I played my Indigenous flute and relived my experiences from over the years.

My anxiety disorder still shows up from time to time, but I do not have to use tranquilizers to cope with it. I had slowly weaned myself off them after my courage journey. Through counseling, I eventually convinced myself that I would live through the anxiety attacks. I navigate my fears and challenges by thinking of Chipeta's endurance and adaptability. When I'm afraid, I tell myself to be Warrior Woman. Now I allow myself to feel my fear. I acknowledge it and reassure myself that I will be taken care of. I know I am capable.

Not *all* tribal members I met over the years adored me. But collaborating with the various tribes taught me about the human cost of prejudice, entitlement, and ignorance. It taught me about perseverance and courage, plus it empowered me to accept who I was and to accept other cultures as they are. I learned a great deal—and I am still learning.

I find beauty in diversity and in the gifts of learning about other cultures. I believe in the end that we are all connected by the matter we are made of. My Indigenous friends and scientists tell us every human being and living creature, the earth and its plants and rocks, and rivers and streams, carry the same basic elements of life found in the stars. What a beautiful thought. Those are the sentiments I put into my paintings. I paint the energy I feel when I consider these very things.

In early December 2020, I started going through boxes containing at least thirty years of journals that held my untold stories and my anguish, my guilt and my grief, my anger, my joys, and my dreams. I had always planned to keep them for my children, so they would know the real deal about my life and times. But after prayerful consideration, I knew I needed to shred it. I pulled out my shredder and spent days shredding page after page of my life. I kept my journals from 2000 to 2015, though, to refer to while I wrote this book. It was a strange sensation to see my life's stories sliced up this way.

I filled several trash bags with "my past," then selected handfuls of shreds from different bags, to use in two pieces of art. Self-portraits, as it were. Then I put a large batch of shreds in one plastic storage bin and threw the bags in the trash. I was truly letting go of the past.

On December 31, I carried the storage bin of saved shreds from my studio to the kitchen. Then I went back downstairs to get a bundle of sage, some sweet grass, and tobacco to burn in our clay fire pit on our deck. The sun was getting ready to set, so it seemed a fitting time to release the pages into the cosmos. By the time I had gotten back upstairs, Mark had moved the fire pit to the center of the deck and put the shreds in it. Mark lifted its lid, and I laid the sage, sweetgrass, and tobacco on the paper. Without a word Mark handed me the lighter. I lit the bundles and the paper, and sweet-smelling smoke rose into the air. Mark carefully put the lid back on. We stood side by side, holding hands and watching the past disappear. My resentment toward Mark floated away with the smoke, and I told him I forgave him for the times he had hurt me. I said I hoped he would forgive me for the times I had hurt him. Flames devoured the paper and, just like that, more than thirty years of my written history was gone. I felt buoyant and full of happiness.

***New life emerged from the ashes of my life.* 2021.**

By spring, the ashes in the fire pit had been snowed and rained on and had congealed into a mat of charcoal and scraps of paper. In the middle of it, tender green tendrils reached toward the sun, because seeds from our bird feeder had fallen in there. Fresh and full of promise, new life had sprouted from the ashes of my life's story. It was a gift to Mark and me, a reminder that life is a series of beginnings and endings, of receiving and letting go. No matter how old we would grow, we could empower each other to live authentically.

August of 2008:

It took me a long time to start thinking about Chipeta. It was almost 16 months before I could write her name in my journal. When I re-read the pages, I realized I had been preparing physically, mentally, and spiritually for my journey. I was in an unfamiliar territory, and I needed to release other issues before embracing Chipeta and her life. I was afraid!

I am suddenly reminded of the time at Chalk Creek when my sister and I were playing at the edge of a small pond in front of our cabin. We were bare except for our cotton panties. Little tin cups were dipped in and out of the water, the tin making a satisfying sound when it scraped the gravel bed of the pond. Then, in a moment, I remembered running across the bridge with a sibling, only to be knocked off and into the pond. Perhaps I was three or so. I could not swim. I landed on my back in the icy water, gasping the moment I hit the surface. My little body floated on the current like an aspen leaf when it drops from the tree in autumn. I cannot remember fear at all. Just a vivid recollection of towering aspen and pine trees arching up into the bright blue sky, sunlight filtering through the paper-thin aspen leaves.

The beauty was extraordinary. I could not hear my siblings, only the current of the creek as it moved through its cobbled bed and into the pond. I was suspended in that time and place, my body slowly drifting into the pond's center, gently turning. Then, I cannot explain it, I was lifted out of the water and set onto the red flagstone patio at the water's edge. I was cold and my teeth chattered. The heat-soaked stones warmed me, and I sat in the sun to dry off.

Where had this memory come from? The whole incident was just a few moments, yet there wasn't any passing of time when I lay in the water. I was just a leaf—part of the tree, part of the Earth, part of something huge. I had guardians then who knew me and watched over me. They knew my purpose in this world long before I could ever imagine what that would be. Our souls know, however, and our lives prepare us for our individual journeys. Even an insignificant event is a preparation for the soul's growth.

I am amazed whenever I re-read this journal entry. I now know I was linked to the cosmos and the spiritual world long before my birth. When I played in the meadows near our family's cabin, I knew the Ancestors were in the trees watching over me. Somewhere along the way, I had lost this connection. It would take me a long time to reunite with my spiritual being and those who had kindly guided me.

The whole time I worked on Chipeta's book, I was convinced I was on Earth to help keep Chipeta's history alive. Perhaps I was but it took me twenty years to realize that it was Chipeta who came to save *me*... from myself. Writing her story split me wide open and expanded my mind and understanding of Indigenous cultures. I had traveled two disparate roads. One was Chipeta's, the other, mine. I would examine my life and the way in which I related to the world. I would reach deep inside myself and rescue the courageous woman who had known who she was. Both roads eventually merged into one, leading me to wholeness. I felt inspired because of my experiences, and it makes its way into my artwork. I have a deep sense of contentment and gratitude for all that I have been blessed with.

It had been more than a decade since I had visited Montrose. My vision is impaired, and my right eye has permanently been blocked with a frosted lens on my eyeglasses. This helps alleviate the double and distorted vision. I still have eye pain, vertigo, and health issues, but I am grateful I can still see to paint. Despite these challenges, the years have not been idle or changeless. During this time, I have painted like crazy, taken care of my granddaughter, Maia (born in 2011), and, later, her twin brothers, Marshall, and Andrew (born in 2014).

In July 2021, our three-year-old grandson, Oliver, whom we had welcomed in 2017, had his third open heart surgery for hypoplastic left heart syndrome. In the past fifteen years, my father passed away, as did Mark's parents, our sister-in-law, and Mark's brother—another of my mentors. And I worked on this book.

In mid-June 2022, Mark and I had just returned from a trip to Montrose, where we hung more than twenty-five of my new paintings in the Ute Indian Museum. It had been twelve years since I had last stepped across the museum's threshold. As soon as I walked through the doors, I felt I had come home again. I was certain my paintings were where they belonged. The timing seemed right. In August 2022, I came back to the museum to speak about my experiences writing about Chipeta and talking about my artwork.

I still communicate with my Indigenous friends from many tribes, though not as often as I would like. I try to stay in touch with CJ, Roland, members of their families, and the Ute Indian Museum. We share a bond—love and appreciation for Chipeta and the Ute culture and its traditions.

Chipeta's name is tattooed on my right shoulder, just above a hummingbird (symbolizing our connection between Heaven and Earth), and the word "believe." There are five stars reminding me of the losses I had, and two symbols one for "spirit" and one "to speak." This tattoo is a permanent reminder of my unforgettable journey and that I will always carry Chipeta's spirit and story with me.

When people ask about my tattoo, I will always share my knowledge about the life and times of this incredible woman. I look forward to the next of many times when I will say, like Chipeta did, "Come children, let me tell you a story."

The Storyteller. **Artwork by Vickie Leigh Krudwig. 2021**

About the Author

Vickie Leigh Krudwig

Vickie is a native of Colorado Springs, Colorado and grew up learning about Ute history at an early age. During her childhood she explored and played in Garden of the Gods Park where the Ute people visited. She watched Ute drummers and dancers perform in Manitou Springs, Colorado, and hunted arrowheads on the plains east of her childhood home, and in the mountains near Salida and Buena Vista, Colorado. A dream in April 2000, led Vickie to write a book about Chipeta, a Ute woman who was born near Conejos, Colorado in 1843.

Her book, *Searching for Chipeta: The Story of a Ute and her People,* was the 2005 winner of the Mountains and Plains Booksellers Association Award for best young people's chapter book. Vickie has talked to thousands of children about Colorado's history, and about Chipeta, wife of Chief Ouray, and the Ute, and other Indigenous tribes who once inhabited the eastern plains of Colorado. Following the release of her award-winning book, *Searching for Chipeta* in 2004, Vickie produced the book, *We are the Noochew: A Brief History of the Ute and their Colorado Connection*, some of which would eventually find its way into the 2018 Fourth Grade Resource Guide Nuu~Ciu Strong—a comprehensive resource guide for teacher's use in the classrooms throughout Colorado.

Vickie also collaborated directly with the Southern Cheyenne and Southern Arapaho tribes of Oklahoma to produce four books for tribal children ages Pre-K-6th grade in 2007-2008. She presented, *Preservation through Print: Preserving Your Tribal History through Self-Publishing*, at the National Indian Education Association in 2005 and to several tribes in El Reno, Oklahoma in July 2007, and again at the National Indian Education Association convention in Oklahoma City in December 2007.

Today, Vickie is an ambassador for Friends of the Ute at the Ute Indian Museum. When Vickie is not writing, she creates artwork based upon her experiences collaborating with Indigenous communities. She supports cultural programming through the sales of her fine art inspired by her experiences over the past twenty years.

To learn more about the Ute History visit:

www.UteIndianMuseum.org

https://www.southernute-nsn.gov

https://www.utemountainutetribe.com/

https://www.utetribe.com/

To see more of Vickie's fine art visit her website at:

www.harmonyhousestudio.com

or

Visit her Facebook page at:

Harmony House Art Studio by Vickie Leigh Krudwig

Acknowledgements

This book is dedicated to my loving and steadfast husband, and best friend, Mark, our children, Jessica (Doug), Rebecca (Alex), Benjamin, and our grandchildren Maia, Andrew, Marshall, and Oliver. I am grateful to friends, old and new, for their love and support .

Thank you to my parents, George and Alice, who became my champions for my work, and to my siblings, Valorie (Garry), Veronica (Gary), George (Cheryl), and Kathrine (John) who all helped me navigate the changes in my life making my world rich and beautiful!

Lastly, this book is a token of my gratitude for Chipeta, who visited me just before dawn in April 2000, turning my life upside down and helped me find my voice, and healing through art and writing. To Chipeta's long gone Ancestors and the Ute people, who were generous in their knowledge and friendship over these many years.

To my many indigenous friends I've made along the way, thank you for sharing your histories, knowledge, and guidance.

To Susan Hill-Newton, Faye Quam-Heimrl, Pat Hayward, and Lauren Springer, Jessica Lindell, Benjamin Krudwig, and Alma Evans for your faith in my project.

For Frank Lloyd Kramer, Kent Douglas, who left us way to soon. Thank you for your encouragement and belief in my book in its very beginning.